To Tony,
Thank you for
being an early
reader of this book.

Robert E Brd

Nov. 13, 2019

Down to Earth

A Novel of New Spiritual Dimensions

by Robert E. Brown

"For love is heaven, and heaven is love."
Sir Walter Scott

Published in the United States of America by:

Robert E. Brown

Copyright © 2019

Printed and bound in the United States of America

ISBN: 978-0-359-99430-4

Cover and book layout design by Robert E. Brown

Table of Contents

Author's Note

Every single person who has lived, is living now and who will live in the future, will come to the end of their life on Earth. Then what? Whether you believe in the continuing of life in the eternal spirit world or not, this story could challenge your belief system.

"Down to Earth" is a novel written from a unique perspective, from characters in heaven sharing about their efforts to create the technology to reach people on Earth giving us a direct view of the spirit world. The main characters are people who lived on the Earth at some time, some died recently and some hundreds or even thousands of years ago.

We have been warned in the past to not have any contact with people who have passed into the spirit realms as any connection was condemned as dabbling in the occult. These warnings were necessary because it is not easy to discern whether one is dealing with a relatively good spirit or an evil one that is masquerading as a benevolent one. To purposely connect with the spirit world should always only be done with sincere prayer and humility.

But what if the spirit world has now progressed to where there are many very high spirits who want to help this world and are reaching out to us. I believe this is true, that at this time in history God is reaching out to the Earth through some very high spirits. All of these spirits are people who once lived on Earth and so naturally there are many who are deeply concerned with our progress.

Unfortunately, using mediums to actively receive or give messages to the spirit world has great limitations. Depending on the skill and spiritual level of the medium, what spirits they attract, and their interpretation of the communication they receive the message may or may not be clear and trustworthy and it is always second hand and filtered information. The greatest obstacle to mass education about the spirit world through mediums is most people don't believe in what happens in séances or "sittings" and so the influence is highly diminished and localized.

Imagine how much ignorance and fear of our afterlife could be alleviated if we could communicate directly with the spirit world in a way that everyone can see and hear together. That is the inspiration for this book.

The spirit world is, without exception, everyone's destination so wouldn't it be empowering to have some idea what to expect when we leave our physical lives. It is my hope that this story will help open the mind to a broader perspective, new possibilities, and reaffirmations of what is important in life, but also be an entertaining read for you.

The descriptions of the spirit world in "Down to Earth" come from my research through many publications. Some of the books I have read were directed through mediums from the world of spirits to let us know they continue to live, what their lives are like and their many activities (see my recommended book list). "Down to Earth" is solely based on my understanding and convictions. I apologize to God, people on Earth, in the spirit world and all creation for any mistakes or mischaracterizations of the Spirt World, of the goals of the higher realms, of the different levels, of the way people interact or behave. None was intentional. This is a book of fiction, but with a hopeful outlook.

Note: There are several characters in this book who are people who lived and have passed into the spirit world including; Jean Baptiste Joseph Fourier who was a scientist who helped Napoleon, Thomas Edison, Nikola Tesla, Albert Einstein, Beethoven, Handel, Bach, Qieci, Kublai Khan, Niccolo Polo, Maffeo Polo, Marco Polo, Dr. Henry Ware, Rev. George Whitefield, Eula Beal, George Harrison (of the Beatles fame) and the three former Popes, St. Gregory I (Gregorius; 590-604), Pius IX (Giovanni Maria Mastai-Ferretti; 1846-78)11 and Pope John Paul II (Karol Józef Wojtyla;1978-2005), Ali ibn Abi Talib (600 – 661), Muhammad ibn Mūsā al-Khwārizmī (780 – 850), and Avicenna Ibn Sīnā (980 – 1037) but how they are used in this story is a product of my imagination. All other characters are invented for the story.

Forward

by David and Takeko Hose
Authors of "Every Day God"

No question, all of us living throughout the countless generations of our humanity have pondered the meaning and nature of "our/my existence". Are we simply here on this planet for a few decades to then return to the ground, leaving but memories behind. Is our existence and story ended when the body no longer functions? The queries, "Who am I?" or, "Why am I here?" have riddled both the nameless person on the street and the greatest minds in our civilizations. Many will address these questions with personal reflections that come and go in conversations; "Well, maybe someday we'll all know." But how?

This past spring I received a phone call from Robert Brown, the author of this book. Truth be told, I'd never met Robert before, but he was interested in a book I had coauthored. My wife and I had written a book, "Every Day God," published in 2000 about our experiences with what some may call a 'higher power,' or God,' after my wife barely survived a gunshot wound in a freakish accident with our son. As we shared, our discussion moved very naturally into spiritual topics. Robert mentioned that he had written a novel, called "Down to Earth," dealing with the spiritual realm and its relationship with people living on earth. This immediately lit my curiosity, since Robert sounded like someone who had a long-standing passion for spiritual knowledge and for a greater understanding of what some call the "afterlife." He agreed to send me a copy. In short, I found this novel fascinating and, unlike anything I'd ever read.

I've been impressed with Robert's background in studying the realm of spirit. At a time in his early teenage years (14), when most young men find a passion for cars, girls and sports, Robert found Christianity and Jesus via a Methodist Revival experience in Oxnard, California. Subsequently, after joining a Christian club in high school and for several years visiting many Christian churches and denominations, Robert concluded that he needed a broader perspective in his relatively young faith. Not content to focus on the Christian realm alone and setting off on what was definitely a road less traveled for one so youthful, he opened his doors to the study of eastern as well as western traditions. Among these, he speaks of Tibetan Buddhism, yoga, and his studies of past-life regression and reincarnation. As years passed into adulthood, of particular interest in Robert's ongoing research were Anthony Borgia's series on "Life in the World Unseen," the works of Emanuel Swedenborg, and "A Wanderer in the Spirit Lands" by A. Farnese.

These books, along with many others received through spiritual mediums and also testimonies from people who had near-death experiences, speak of the spirit realm as a place of mountains, trees, homes, gardens, birds and animals, music, laughter, friends, purposeful occupations, and pleasurable hobbies and passions; briefly, all that we on earth experience and yet far more beautiful and amazing. Because of these amazing realizations about the spirit world, Robert felt he needed to write a book, and to write it from the spirit world perspective.

All in all, the world of spirit represents a different and finer dimension than our physical senses are able to perceive. Yet the great spiritual masters and "seers" of history speak of our essence as "spirit" and of the spiritual senses that dwell deep in the heart and being of each one of us, as natural as our physical arms and legs. Is it then enough to dismiss the reality of what some have named our 'higher selves,' or the existence of other dimensions in this universe? It brings to mind what many of the great spiritual teachings have stated, "You are not your body," or, that we are each a microcosm of a multi-dimensional universe.

The interesting thing about Robert's book, "Down to Earth" is that it doesn't claim to be the result of mediumship or channeling and isn't merely describing the spiritual 'landscape' or phenomena of the spiritual realm. It is a present day story, written from the first person perspective from a group in the spirit world celebrating and recounting their efforts and success to reach mankind through a new technology that opens a visual and audio connection with the spirit world. The trajectory of the story goes through the initial breakthrough with a few scientists to a popular TV show revealing Heaven to the Earthly audience, then on to a stadium with a worldwide audience showing people who were extensively reported as dying now speaking to the world from the spirit world.

The book shows the spirit group meeting and deciding on different approaches to each of the major religions and how to educate them of the spirit world through a sensitive and effective effort.

The next stage shows the group working with their Earthly counter-parts to create a webpage where the spirit group shows videos of many aspects of spirit world, the higher and the lower levels, along with an-swering questions from Earth viewers. Finally the Earth side opens spirit centers around the world where people can come to talk with loved ones who have passed to the other side.

Robert has done an impressive amount of homework in history, as you'll see. A slew of historic incidents and events are sewn together as figures within the spirit world are able to meet those on earth via a large screen, meaning family members, friends, even opponents who know of or were a part of their lives. A memorable example is the young Buddhist monk who committed suicide by immolating himself in protest of these new spirit world messages, only to find himself in the spiritual realm being soothed by loving people seeking to cool and soothe his spirit. He tearfully warns those gathered to see him on the screen not to make his same mistake, and that there are better ways.

However, still to be accomplished is the ultimate spiritual evolution, and consequent revolution, of humankind itself. The book speaks of an age literally beyond belief, but of a leap forward into genuine con-sciousness of the eternal quality of our life, via these spiritual/physical transmissions and communications, the results and consequences of our actions on earth, both positive and negative, and the path of spiritual de-velopment from the lowest and most ignorant bestial state to that of di-vine wisdom and love. *(To add my own opinion here, it's my conviction that in a very real way, Robert Brown has been inspired, in part beyond his own ideas, to write this novel, by those who touched him in spirit to reach out to anyone ready to consider its message.)

This past weekend saw the horrific mass shooting nightmares in El Paso, Texas and Dayton, Ohio. As I sit here in this quiet room consider-ing an answer to all of this meaningless insanity and tragedy. Honestly, it brings me right back to Robert's book. What would it mean for our humanity to discover without doubt our ultimate and timeless destina-tion? In my thought it would throw a powerful and unprecedented light into a world of questions about who we are and why we're here. Yes, it is a novel, but it offers a beam that deserves and asks for openness and reflection on the part of its readership."

Acknowledgments

My first thanks go to God, our Heavenly Parent, for the love and vision He/She has poured into creation, creating our Earthly lives where we meet and have to overcome hardships to grow our character and then giving us a place to live eternally in the spirit world, as co-creators, sons and daughters.

My second thanks go to those in the spirit world who inspired this book. I don't know who you are yet, but look forward to meeting you some day. With their inspiration, I knew I wanted to write a book, a book about spirit world, and written from the spirit side perspective.

Thanks for my wife, Penny, and my family for putting up with my passion for the spirit world and giving me more books on related subjects to add to my overall view of our spiritual lives.

The original manuscript for "Down to Earth" was written from 2015 to 2016 taking about a year to write, and then..., nothing happened. No one, that I could find, was interested in reading it. One friend, Caroline Cecile did some early editing and came up with the name: "Down to Earth." Then early in 2019, reaching out to David and Takeko (Tacco) Hose in a phone call to talk about their own book, "Every Day God", David asked if I had ever written anything. I told him about "Down To Earth" and later sent him a PDF of the book. They were very excited about my book and shared it with friends. Suddenly the book had a life. I am profoundly grateful to David and Tacco Hose.

The early readers of the book are Matthew Morrison, Tony Aparo, Claire Bowles and Caroline Cecile. They each gave me pointers on how to improve the story. Matthew Morrison, especially gave me a detailed examination of the book with some suggestions.

Clarie Bowles introduced me to Joy Pople, who became the Editor of "Down to Earth", and whose input has been invaluable to help bring the novel alive, flowing, consistent and readable.

Thanks to all who had a part in bringing this book to life.

Chapter 1
Daniel and Martha

Daniel Everheart
1749, Long Island, New York

It was a balmy August day in the northern part of Hempstead Town, in the Colony of New York. I took the steps slowly, with my arms tied behind my back. Today, especially, I didn't want to stumble. The wooden steps and the platform were newly made for this day, but they creaked, nevertheless. In the village square, I could hear sea birds off the Long Island Sound mocking me.

A voice, familiar to me as Constable Stu Mackle, spoke clearly, "Daniel Everheart, you have been found guilty of the Satanic practice of divination and working with the occult to contact the dead. You are condemned to hang by the neck until you are dead. As the good book demands in Deuteronomy 18:10-12 you must be purged and I quote: 'There shall not be found among you … anyone who practices divination or tells fortunes or interprets omens, or a sorcerer or a charmer or a medium or a necromancer or one who inquires of the dead, for whoever does these things is an abomination to the LORD. And because of these abominations the LORD your God is driving them out before you.'"

Another voice, my accuser, Reverend Sebastian Marshall, an elder minister of our Congregational Church who used to be my mentor and I thought my friend, said simply with his eyes never leaving mine, "May God have mercy on your soul."

I begged my wife to not attend as I didn't want her to be implicated with me, but I could see her in the back of the crowd holding our infant son, with tears flowing down her cheeks.

Perhaps fearing that I would lay a curse on my accusers they didn't ask if I had any last words. The young man, my executioner, I knew from helping set fence posts on my small acreage, placed a black cloth bag over my head and led me to the center of the platform. I heard someone call out, "Devil worshipper!" and many projectiles struck me while others cursed me with similar accusations. The heavy noose was secured around my neck and they tightened the rope. I could smell the hemp rope and the sweat of the executioner, along with my own fear.

Silently I cried out to God, "Lord God, I didn't mean to do harm or to sin against you. I only wanted to use the gifts you gave me to help people grieving for their loved ones. Have mercy on me! Have mercy on my wife and son!" I let out a sob and felt the trap door below spring open and I dropped through. My throat jerked shut and suddenly I was above the scene looking down at a man being hung with a crowd gathered. I felt no pain, in fact, I felt better than I had in years. I looked at the man dangling, swaying with his feet twitching and recognized his home spun clothes as my own. What was happening to me? I called out to people I knew, but no one paid me any attention. Then I saw my wife and son. Why was she crying? "Martha, I'm here! I'm feeling fine. The rope must have broken. Martha!" I yelled. She ignored me, and turning, walked away weeping. "Martha!"

Then I saw the strangest thing, my father who had died years before of consumption came over to me and said, "Daniel, no one can hear you. You are no longer part of the world. Come with me, there are many friends and family waiting for you." I looked at him with my mouth open, "Dad?" Then I sat down and wept.

Martha's Passing

The small cottage was dimly lit and smoky with a cedar log fire in the small rusty fireplace. Dr. Emmit Henderson who had been in the house for the last hour bent over Martha to check her pulse. Martha, her once beautiful blond hair, now gray, matted. A smile came to Martha's pale, sickly face and she called out, "Daniel!"

She could see me! Tears came to my eyes. The doctor looked scandalized knowing how I died and not wanting to be partner to connecting with the departed.

My father had been there for my passing and also I would welcome Martha, my beloved, to her new home. Although I had been living in the spirit world for the last thirty five years I also witnessed my wife and son's lives. Often I would watch over them and at times I knew my wife could feel my presence, although she cautiously kept that knowledge to herself.

It was June, 1784 and the war for independence from England was now over for almost a year. As a poor widow the war years had been very hard on Martha, especially living in the battleground colony of

New York. She became a washer woman along with being a nanny for a wealthy loyalist family in the newly established, North Hempstead. The family now fearfully kept to themselves having been supporters of the crown. They set Martha up in a small cottage on their land so she could be available for the family's four children along with running errands and shopping for them to help maintain their seclusion.

I watched as her poor emaciated sweaty body trembled, her eyes glazed over and then rolled back in her head. There was a rattling gasp and her body went still. Presently I watched as her spirit came out of the top of her head and then my lovely wife stood before me. She was confused and looking around. She was no longer a haggard older graying woman, old beyond her years from privation. Now, seeing me and realizing what had just happened, the young Martha I had left all those years ago stood there beaming. Her blond hair fine and silky, her blue grey eyes full of life once again.

"She's gone," the doctor declared. The lady of the house looked over and nodded.

"She was good to us and will be missed. She will be buried on our land though separate from my family plot," the lady declared. "When can you pick up the body?"

But these were no longer our affairs. "Martha, how I longed for this day," I exclaimed and we hugged each other, tears flowing.

"Daniel," she proclaimed. "Daniel," and she sighed. "Our son, Samuel…"

"I know," and put my fingers to her lips.

Little did I know how our now tranquil lives would forever change as we were soon to be invited to join a grand adventure that would last for hundreds of years.

Daniel and Martha Everheart

New York Colony, Daniel: 1720 to 1749 and Martha: 1725 to 1784

My name is Daniel Everheart and along with my wife, Martha, this is our story of helping an amazing organization in the spirit world reach out to the modern world to give hope and vision and a unified message.

I had always been a man of great passion and also open to spirit influences and both of these attributes combined was the reason I was put to death in 1749 in the New York colony. From when I was a young lad I could hear and sometimes see the departed spirits. I became more sensitive to what people were thinking and could experience their suffering and I felt this was a gift from God. But the colonies were going through turbulent times in agitation with England and King George and few had the patience to deal with a firebrand talking with the dead.

Our pastor, Reverend Sebastian Marshall, became more alarmed as I shared my gift of sensitivity, until finally he turned against me and went to the magistrate.

My desire was only to help others, to calm the bereaved, to bring comfort to those who had passed by connecting them to those remaining on the Earth side. When my father met me at my passing he brought me to a lush land, beautiful, green with flowers all around. There was a lovely cottage, similar to my home on Earth, but more vibrant. Everything was so alive and fresh. There were friends there who had passed before me and my sister who I loved dearly who died as a child of twelve being thrown from a horse. While on Earth I was very aware of departed spirits talking about their new life in the spirit lands and yet I could not have begun to imagine this incredible place that was my new home.

My loving wife, Martha, left on Earth was also sensitive to other world influences though not as attuned as I was. When it became apparent that I would not win my case I urged her to denounce my experiences so as to not suffer the same fate as me. But tragically this left her impoverished with our infant son to raise when she was denied the right to inherit my land. It was with great joy to welcome her into these beautiful lands at her passing and we have stayed just as close as we had been as husband and wife on Earth.

Our son, Samuel, who grew up without his father, unfortunately, did not turn out so well. Samuel joined the red coats at first and later helped the colonists, but his loyalties were always suspect. It was not that he was influenced by the wrong kind of men, but rather he organized and led a small band of thieves and cut throats who played whichever side paid better. In the end he was shot during a failed attempt by his gang to rob a convoy bringing supplies to the Continental Army in Germantown, New York. He arrived in the spirit realms two years before Martha, but I decided to wait for Martha before beginning to reach out to him, since he had no connection to me.

It has been Martha's passion to help our son rise from the wretched level he resides in here in the spirit realms. It is usually a slow and agonizing path to grow in the lowest spirit realms. Once a person realizes he or she can't blame anyone else for their situation and repent for the harm they have caused while living on earth, they can begin to take responsibility and correct their mistakes. Though Martha and I would be given many responsibilities I would help her reach out to our lost son in the blackest hell.

Through the years we watched America grow from a few colonies of mostly rural farmers with a few bigger cities to a strong nation from the Atlantic to the Pacific. I say we watched this progress, but like most in the spirit realms it was not full time as I was also occupied with my passions along with my own growth and development in my eternal home. I entered the spirit realms, as I said, at a good level, but it was by far not the highest realm. I have made some progress from where I began in these last 250 years, or so.

In the spirit realms you will gravitate to others who are at the same level as you are and also to people who have the same interests. Because while on Earth I was very interested in connecting people on Earth to people in spirit I was naturally drawn to a group of people who are working to bridge the two realms. It was while Martha and I were learning how to welcome new people to the spirit lands at their passing that we were approached by a couple, shining splendidly and with dazzling smiles with a depth of love that cannot be faked here. It was about fifty years after Martha had joined me in these lands.

"Daniel and Martha, I am Garuda and this is my wife, Rajinda and we have been watching your growth in this realm and we would like to invite you to join us in our work," said a man of dark skin. We were aware of the American native and also of the people brought from Africa as slaves, but could not tell where this man was from while on Earth. He could see our intrigued expressions and continued with a smile, "We are from what is now the continent of India, though it was not called that in our day. We have been in the spirit lands for several thousand years."

"We are pleased to meet you and how can we help you?" Martha asked.

"How would you like to help us communicate on a large scale with the people on Earth without using mediums?" Rajinda said. "We are part of an organization that is working to create the machines that will allow us to do that."

And that was the beginning of an incredible journey.

Now over two hundred years later, scientists have created computers and the way they speak to each other, the Internet. I am not a scientist and don't understand how any of these things work. The overall group that Garuda and Rajinda lead is called Jiva Satata, which is a phrase in Sanskrit, Jiva meaning spirit and Satata uninterrupted or eternal. When we learned more about this group, we felt honored to be asked to join this auspicious organization. Jiva Satata is made up of former mediums, like I was, along with scientists, engineers, inventors, former politicians, some very religious people, not just Christians but from many other religions who were always looking for deeper truths, and a lot of people who want to open communications for more personal reasons.

One amazing thing I have gleaned from life here is people are much more interested in dogma and religion than God is. I have met very high spirits who were Hindu or Buddhist and who lived pure and sacrificial lives full of love. And also I have seen that not all Christians end up in high levels or even in heaven, depending on how they treated their fellow man. God, I found, was more interested in the heart of man, how he treated others, his sincerity, humility than words professed.

Now that the technology is ready Jiva Satata's strategy is to reach some scientists who are already spiritually inclined on Earth and together with our scientists in spirit world perfect the way to communicate between the spirit and physical worlds. What everyone knows who lives in the world of spirit is that the spirit world is just as substantial and real as the physical world. It is just on a much higher vibration level of energy. That means it should be possible to make the technology to bridge these two levels of vibration.

This book is a recounting of what happened when this amazing organization in the spirit world was able to open communication with people living on Earth.

Chapter 2
First Contact

Electronic Connection to the Earth Side

"Hello,
Hello,
Can you hear this?"

Edwin Jackson was a physicist who had worked in computer silicone chip design first for IBM in the earlier years and later for Micro Sun International. But he was also involved in the spiritualist movement, more as a dabbler. He had received some images in his mind from his mother, but was never sure if it was real or not. Edwin's fellow scientists would not be impressed with his interest in connecting to the dead, so he mostly kept that to himself. His mother had been everything to him and he took her death hard.

Edwin had tried to reach his mom through a local spiritualist/palm reader but felt it was contrived and had been a waste of his money. Later he attended a renowned medium on tour and while in the audience the medium said someone's mother was there and mentioned blue roses. Blue Roses had been the name of his mother's ladies' fine clothing store in Brooklyn. Edwin felt an electric current run up his spine and as the revelations continued verifying that it was actually his mom, he broke down. He then began Googling about movements that try to contact the spiritual realms and learned about the Spiritualist movement. He located a Spiritualist church in the bay area of California, The Spiritualist Church of Two Worlds, in Old San Leandro and began attending services. Their services were held in a simple tan L shaped building across from a BART station.

In the spirit world, we had been trying to reach Edwin by voice through his computer speakers by varying the vibrational output at a much denser level than our world and were beginning to see something come through. Edwin thought it was static and brought his Apple computer in for repair. Of course, Fry's Electronics in Fremont could not find any problems.

Finally on October 21st, 2020, we had a substantial breakthrough. Mr.

Jackson was at home in Castro Valley working on a balsa wood model of the Golden Gate Bridge, one of his several hobbies, and at the same time listening to his classic rock music selection through Pandora on his computer. We had Edwin's mother, Shirley Jackson, join us a few days earlier as we felt a breakthrough was coming and wanted her to be the first to make verbal contact with her son.

As Creedence Clearwater Revival was singing, "Fortunate Son" there was a static hiss, the music was interrupted, then silence, then in a tinny drawn out voice,

"Hello, Edwin! Ed, can you hear me? It's your Mom," came through, broken and barely audible. Edwin dropped his hot glue gun and the piece of wire representing the bridge cables he was holding. The glue gun hit his leg, burned him and he let out a yelp. "What? What is going on here?"

"Can you hear me?"

Edwin went over to his computer and said, "Who is this? Have you hacked into my system?"

He then heard a man's voice, "Please speak into the microphone and turn up your speakers all the way."

"Who is this?" Edwin demanded.

"We can barely hear you, sir, please speak into your microphone. We have a lot to tell you and you may find it hard to believe at first."

"Edwin, this is Mom. Yes, I am still dead, or really very much alive, but dead to the physical world."

Edwin's voice broke as he said, "What? What is this? Mom? How is this possible? Is this really you?"

"Yes, love, it's me."

"How do I know this is my Mom?"

"Recently you went to hear the medium, John Edward, at the Oakland auditorium and you were told I was reaching out to you there. You have been attending The Spiritualist Church of Two Worlds and though you are sensitive you have not developed your spiritual senses yet. I did send you an image of you and your sister when we visited Berkeley campus for her graduation. Didn't you see that in your mind?"

"Mom?" Edwin choked out, tears beginning to fill his eyes.

"Yes, love."

The man spoke up again,

"Edwin, we are an organization in the spirit world, or you might say heaven, although that is a very simplistic word and barely describes the incredibly vast and complex world on this side. We have been working for many years to develop communication between the Earthly world and the spirit world. Actually our work began first with our inventions of the telephone, radio, then television, and now with computers as steps toward developing this inter-realm communication. My name is Joseph Fourier, a scientist like you, but who lived a few hundred years ago, actually during Napoleon's time. We have other scientists, engineers, former mediums and some people who have always longed to open communication between the two realms in our organization. We chose to work with you because you are a computer scientist and also interested in the spirit world. What do you think?"

"Uhhh… I don't know. Wow! Is this real?" Edwin stammered. "Incredible!"

"Yes, sir, it is very real and frankly we are as excited as you are. This is, as you say, incredible. We have been working for this for a long time, as I said earlier."

"Wow! Unbelievable! Wait a minute, did you say you created the telephone, radio, television and computers?"

"Almost all inventions were first created in the spirit world and then we find a compatible person interested in that field on Earth and begin to guide them through inspiration, intuition and sometimes through dreams to develop the Earthly version of the invention," Joseph explained. "But we are happy for that inventor to be credited with the invention. We have no need for wealth or fame here. Later when the inventor passes he or she joins our growing numbers of creative people to help mankind progress."

Joseph Fourier had lived an exciting life, assisting Napoleon along with the 200 savants in his campaigns to Egypt as his scientific advisor and was appointed Secretary of the Institut d'Égypte and later in France as Prefect (Governor) of the Department of Isère in Grenoble and as professor at École Polytechnique. Later in life his was appointed as Permanent Secretary of the French Academy of Sciences.[1] Joseph's specialty was mathematics, heat transference and vibrations, both became foundations for his later work with scientists in the 20th and 21st centuries in developing computers from the spirit world side. Joseph joined with Jiva Satata soon after entering the spirit world.

"OK, what do you want me to do?" Edwin said cautiously.

"We need scientists and engineers on Earth to assist us in improving the technology, first with the audio communication, then video." Joseph explained. "I think you can hear the distortion coming through, and we want to clean this up before we move to the more challenging visual transference."

"Well that is not my expertise; I work in computers, but not in the audio or visual side." Edwin explained.

"Yes, we know that, so please find the people who can help. We will get back to you in a month of Earthly time, say on what is known as Thanksgiving in your country with whomever you can bring. Is this good with you?"

"Frankly I'm overwhelmed, and really don't know what to say. But OK, I know some people who might be interested if I can convince them that I am not a nut case."

"It was a pleasure to talk to you, Edwin. We are going to celebrate this victory with a great party. Farewell and we will connect again on Thanksgiving."

Outreach to
Spiritually Sensitive People

For the past two hundred years there has been growing interest from people on Earth to communicate with people in the spirit world using electronic instruments. There was a desire to advance past the need for spiritual mediums that the general public considers just a parlor trick. The early successes were known as EVP or Electronic Voice Phenomenon using sound recording devices to hear spirits trying to communicate. When images are included in the transmission these were known to physic researchers on Earth as ITC or Instrumental Transcommunication.[2] The results so far were crude and unimpressive, not something that could convince skeptical society. Thomas Edison, in an interview with Scientific America, said electronic communication with the spirit world would be a much better way to communicate than with Ouija boards and table tipping.

Our scientists and engineers in the spirit world were working on perfecting this technology so anyone, no matter how spiritually inclined could participate in this trans-realm communication. Jiva Satata was made up of the technical side, those working on making the actual instruments, along with former mediums, religious leaders and spiritual people making up the spiritual side.

Martha and I were asked to lead the spiritual outreach to add to our group those who had been mediums or spiritually sensitive people while alive on Earth who are interested in communication with the Earth.

As technology was leading the world to new horizons people were also becoming more spiritual. A greater number of people all over the world are born with a natural gift of sensitivity to the world of spirit, whether through visions, through audio reception or for most, a deep intuition and a feeling of being led in their lives. We organized hundreds of former mediums in the spirit world, clairvoyants, clairaudients, mystics and sages to identify receptive people on Earth and to share messages that a new age is coming for mankind and that all the walls are coming down.

Connecting audibly in a clear voice through a machine with Edwin was our first substantial scientific breakthrough for the last one hundred and fifty years or so of guiding technology to this momentous day and this called for a grand party.

Chapter 3

Celebration
in Spirit World

The Celebration

A thought communication was sent out to all who had ever partici-pated in our work these last three hundred years, of a great celebration coming soon, for our first major success. Here in the spirit world com-munication over a distance is sent through thought from one person to another. You think of a person and send a thought to them and they can then respond with a returning thought.

Martha and I arrived early to help prepare the atmosphere for the gathering. Martha had been experimenting with creating different pies and pastries and had now created a nectarine and plum pie that she was eager to share.

We went over to greet Anslema Glaus, a slight red headed woman and a longtime friend. "Anslema! So good to see you," Martha hugged her and showing her the pies we brought said, "What do you have planned for the entertainment?"

Anselma Glaus, who was asked to plan the celebration, was from a fourth century village of 200 hundred people in Roman territory that would be part of Southern Germany in the modern era. Her village was at the crossroads of two path connecting different parts of the continent with one passing through the Alps. Although she had been a simple vil-lage woman she had an amazing knack and passion for creating wonder-ful celebrations and was the event planner for Jiva Satata.

"Since this involves people from all over the world and from many ages I decided on classical music with a large orchestra," Anslema de-clared. "Beethoven will be our lead musician who has promised to bring together the best musicians through the ages. Beethoven especially is a master musical architect creating such awe inspiring color structures with his music." Harmonized music in the spirit world creates flowing color structures above the performers of such vibrancy and intensity that they make the best of the aurora borealis on Earth seem like a carni-val light show.[3] These colorful structures are flowing and evolving with the music from a large orchestra that can go way into the sky and last long after the music stops. Many musicians were superb at composition, but not all were also gifted in musical architecture, plus not all types of music lent itself to creating beautiful color structures.

Anslema continued, "Phoenician wine makers were invited who had perfected a wine in the spirit world, famous for the last 3,000 years. I'm sure you've had some of their wine before, and they promised to bring their best." All alcoholic beverages in the spirit world will not make a person intoxicated but instills feelings of pleasant well-being.

"We do love their wine," I said smiling.

"There's more, you'll see," Anslema said with her dimpled grin. "I don't want to ruin it for you."

The celebration was in a beautiful field surrounded by large graceful trees and flowers of all types and in far more colors than are known on Earth. The uplifting fragrances of all the flowers filled the air. I bent down and cupped a daisy in my hand. The flower responded with a quiver of vibration, sparking in beautiful colors and perfume. I thanked this representative flower and felt gratitude from all the flowers around me.

Martha, seeing this exchange remarked, "It is so wonderful that everything responds to love. The flowers are here for our joy and are fulfilled when we notice them and return the beauty they give us with our love."

A stream was flowing across the field full of magnificent scintillating fish of many different colors and was visited by birds that love to interact with the people.

After having a most satisfying meal of pies, cakes, fruit, delicacies and wine we sat with many friends on the grass where we could see the orchestra and choir. The orchestra performed Beethoven's Fifth and Ninth Symphonies along with three he had written in spirit world. These last three were accompanied by the choir with superb sopranos and tenors leading the songs.

"Look at that! Those color structures are amazing!" Martha exclaimed. "I never get tired of the music, the singing and the color, although I'm not generally enthralled with classical music." And as if Anslema had been waiting for this she stood up and proclaimed that we would now have some folk songs along with couple and group dancing. This was more to my liking.

Since not everyone knew Anselma I asked her if she would give a short testimony about her life on Earth.

Anselma said she would be happy to and began, "My home village was in what is now Germany, although at that time it was under Roman rule and I lived from 354 to 400 AD when I died from an infection from a gash in my leg. I certainly had no understanding of life after death, but did have a strong and simple faith in Jesus and God, based on the Roman Catholic Church."

"My family always had sheep and a few goats that we raised to use their wool to dye and spin into yarns that we would sell at the monthly market in the closest village. After living in the spirit world for several hundred years, my life here was very similar to living on earth in my simple village surrounded by forests. I didn't know anything else. I began to become aware that the spirit world was much more vast and complicated than I had known. This came about when a visitor came to our village and began explaining and then bringing those willing to adventure beyond to other parts of the spirit world."

She continued, "In my life on Earth I had married at 17 and was able to give birth to five children, although two died young. But I had a mother's heart and took in some village children who lost their parents to war or sickness. I also loved to recognize these children for their accomplishments and would give all the children extravagant celebrations for each milestone crossed. We also put on performances using local villages for travelers being on a crossroad."

"I was asked to be part of Jiva Satata to bring a motherly heart to the group and also bring my love of celebrations," she said smiling.

Finishing her comments, she added, "We anticipate some real problems on Earth when we open the pathway to communication between the two worlds. I hope I can be of help in those challenging times also."

We all stood up and applauded.

We, who have been in these spirit lands for a long time have to remember our first impressions to be able to share them with you. Here the colors are so vibrant and alive, everything is alive. The air is always clear and fresh; the sun is always above keeping us delightfully warm, there is no day and night, only perpetual sunshine. Life here is a celebration every day, so when we have an official ceremony it is an added joy to see people we know and love or to meet so many new and wonderful people, the air is vibrating with joy and love.

After the celebration continued for a while Anslema stood up and announced, "Everyone, we are being honored by a visit from the leaders of

Jiva Satata. Not everyone has met Garuda and Rajinda so it is my honor to introduce them." We all stood up and applauded as our good friends appeared together holding hands and smiling broadly. These spirits, dark in skin, noble, beautiful, clothed in spirit gowns of scintillating white, Garuda with a golden belt and Rajinda with a violet sash, came from a much higher heaven of the celestial realm. They emit an aura of brilliant golden light and give us a deep feeling of being in the presence of God's overwhelming love. They shared their deep appreciation for everyone's contributions and said from now on our communication with Earth will advance quickly .

No one from our level of heaven, sometimes known as Summerland, could venture into the divine realms without being escorted by a resident. The vibration is so high they would feel like they couldn't breathe without the protective intervention from a divine spirit. This is true for all levels in the spirit world, you can go to a lower realm, but can't travel freely to a higher realm until your spirit is at a level of love through service achieved both from your life on Earth and your work in the spirit world.

The celebration was wonderful, uplifting and what everyone needed. It lasted for many Earth days and Joseph Fourier, Martha, myself and others on the lead staff had to remind ourselves of the passing of the days to be ready for the next planned meeting with Edwin.

Time can easily be forgotten here in the spirit world, as there is no rising and setting sun, no seasons, and no concept of time passing at all. Some spirits are assigned to keep aware of what year and age it is on Earth and especially of coming disasters or great turning events. When a natural disaster or a great conflict is eminent then spirits must be ready and waiting to help the throngs of spirits entering the next phase of their lives in the eternal spirit world and especially if someone they know and love is coming soon. But for billions of spirits whatever is happening on Earth or even what century it is, is of little concern for them. How many hundreds of millions or even billions have been in spirit world for thousands of years already?

Chapter 4
Thanksgiving

A Meeting of Friends

Edwin Jackson, just under six feet tall, dark curly hair, at 42 was in relativily good shape, although his stomach was growing faster than he liked. Edwin lived on a quarter acre plot in a split level home he had commissioned from a local architect. He was really looking forward to this get-together with friends and for the feast, but was uneasy with what was to follow. For this Thanksgiving, November 26, 2020, Edwin had invited some audio, visual and computer engineers and one spiritualist friend, altogether eight people, two couples and four other friends.

The first to arrive were Enrique and Barbara Rodriquez, a Christian couple who had started their own computer repair company three years ago in Union City. Enrique was a handsome third generation Mexican-American and Barbara, a plump, motherly woman of Irish ancestry. "Hey, hello Enrique, Barbara, welcome. Something smells good! What is that?"

"It is my own invention, sweet potato curry stew," Barbara said smiling.

"Oh, yes! That will go well with the turkey I have in the oven," Edwin said, wondering if that was true.

The doorbell rang and Edwin welcomed Jill Tanner, a striking tall black lady and video expert Edwin knew from his years with IBM. Jill came in with two bags full of vegetables. Behind Jill was Ben Stine, a good friend of Edwin from their years together at Stanford pursuing their physics major. Ben, Jewish but not observant, was short at 5' 8" with dark curly hair and glasses.

"Jill! Looks like you brought the whole grocery store. Welcome!" Edwin exclaimed.

"I'll make a salad if I can use your utensils," Jill responded as she headed for Edwin's modern brightly lit kitchen.

"And I brought the essentials, beer!" Ben proclaimed.

"Bring it all in the kitchen. We'll be feasting in an hour or so, so that will give Jill time to make her salad," Edwin said giving Jill a wink. "I'm expecting four more guests. Hold on I think I hear someone coming up the walk."

Jackie Nagorski, average height with short dark hair, was Edwin's friend he had met at a spiritualist church. She had been a great help after his mom passed away. Edwin opened the door and Jackie came in and gave him a hug. "I'm so glad you could make it, Jackie," Edwin said.

"I brought a couple of pies, cherry and apple. What's this all about Edwin, you sounded rather stressed when you called?" Jackie said.

"First we eat, then, well, then we'll see," Edwin replied.

Michael Templeton, founder and CEO of Templeton Technologies came up the walk after parking his classic dark blue 1982 Jaguar XJ6 across the street. Michael looked like a movie-star, dark blond way hair, bright blue eyes. "I picked up some potato salad and cranberry sauce at the deli. Hope you don't mind, I'm no chef."

"That's great, Mike, it will be well received and eagerly devoured, I'm sure. Come in," Edwin said.

Finally the Petersons, Stan and Irene, showed up twenty minutes later. "We had to get a sitter for our twin girls and the sitter was late, so sorry." Stan was of Scandinavian stock, tall, blond, often stern looking while Irene was his opposite complement, short, auburn hair with light brown eyes and usually smiling. Edwin had his fingers crossed with the Petersons. Stan didn't believe in anything spiritual, only what could be proven scientifically. He was an excellent engineer who had several patents for silicone disk growth and hardware interfaces. They both worked for Hewlett Packard, Stan in research and Irene as the local Human Resources Director.

Edwin had just told his friends he was conducting some experiments and needed their help. It was to be a potluck dinner with everyone assigned to bring various dishes that together would be a grand Thanksgiving meal. Edwin supplied the turkey and some wine. He wasn't sure if his spirit friends were going to visit and so he kept everyone in the dark about what his great experiment was. His computer was on but asleep, with the speakers turned all the way up.

The dinner was a happy reunion of friends and it was starting to get later into the evening and Edwin was getting anxious. If nothing happened he might just say it was just a ruse to get all his friends to share Thanksgiving with him. He would have invited everyone out on his deck with the spacious backyard but it was chilly and he needed the computer equipment for his "friends."

Jill broke into the conversations going on around the table. "Well, Edwin, what devilish experiments are you up to? Do you have Franken-stein's monster hiding in your bedroom? Do you need us to help animate him?"

"He's alive!!!!" shouted Ben, who recently joined Edwin as an engineer working at Micro Sun International. Many around the table laughed.

There was an electronic screech from the computer speakers, static and a low hiss. Finally Joseph's familiar voice came through:

"Hello...hello, can you hear us?"

then silence.

Edwin gave a nervous laugh, and said, "You were close about reani-mating the dead back to life. I think I will let them explain it to you."

"Who?" the guests asked in unison. "What's going on?"

Edwin went over to his microphone, and said, "Yes, we can hear you? Are you still there?"

"Wait, we are working on the connection. Are you there? We can't hear you."

Edwin realized the microphone was not turned on and he switched it on. "Yes, we are here. I have gathered some friends who probably can help you with your plans. Please explain to them what this is all about."

Joseph began, "Some of you may accept this after a little while and some may find it unbelievable and will not be comfortable with what I have to say. My name is Joseph Fourier and I died in France in 1830."

There was a stunned silence, then the explosion came and everyone started talking at once. "What? What game are you playing, Edwin? Ha ha, nice joke. Do you have someone broadcasting this nonsense from somewhere else? What is this?"

"I found it hard to believe also. I guess they are from heaven, or some-thing. It is bizarre and at first I thought it was a prank, like you, but then they had my mom come on and speak. And she died last year. But she said things to me that made it clear it was her." Edwin explained rather flummoxed.

Jill fainted. Ben's face turned red, looking like he was going to explode.

Edwin put his head in his hands and implored his friends, "Please everyone, hear Joseph out. Please don't go." Stan, a lifelong atheist, stood up and said, "Is this your latest gimmick to get me to believe in your god, and the mumbo jumbo nonsense you have been spouting about talking to ghosts. I am out of here." And turning with a scowl to his wife,

Irene, said, "Let's go. Party is over. How sad that you would stoop to this new low." The Petersons got up, Irene grabbed her serving bowl with the remainder of the three bean salad, and they marched out of the dining room. Irene looked back and with her lips tight, shrugged her shoulders.

Jackie Nagorski, who Edwin knew from the Spiritualist Church, was looking at Edwin intently with one raised eyebrow. She said, "OK, this is very interesting. I never heard a spirit speak through a computer before."

Before the final couple Enrique and Barbara Rodriquez could put in their response, Joseph began again, "We know this is hard to believe but what we call the spirit world, where everyone who has ever lived on Earth goes to when they die, actually exists. I was a Catholic and it was not anything I would have ever considered, talking to the dead. It was considered occult, devil worship, at worst. But I assure you the spirit world is very real. I am right now with ten others in a room in my house, in what you would call heaven, and most of us are part of a larger group that is working to create a connection from the spirit world to your world through computers."

Joseph may be a brilliant scientist, but he was also someone who liked to talk a lot. Maybe it was a French thing. I was glad that he was the spokesperson.

Jill was revived and Barbara was holding a damp cloth to her forehead. Barbara said, "Enrique and I are strong Christians and we believe in heaven and hell, but I don't know about working with dead people. Kind of gives me the creeps." Enrique added, "How do we know you are not some evil spirits trying to possess us or make us do some weird stuff?"

"Well, I guess we are making some progress, if you believe we are from the spiritual world. I am going to ask Daniel to help with this. Dan?"

Ouch, I guess I spoke too soon. I took hold of the spirit world counterpart to a microphone and began speaking. We don't need telephones or microphones to communicate here, as I explained earlier, all we need to do is think about a person and send a thought to them. These electronic machines gathered around us here were developed to help in our great work in connecting to the physical world.

"Joseph is a scientist who lived during the French Revolution and worked directly with Napoleon. My wife and I were Christians in pre-America, living right before the American Revolution. But we were also sensitive to spirit communication, I was what would now be called a medium. In fact I was brought to the gallows because of this 'gift'. But when I woke up in the spirit world I was not in hell as my pastor assured me I was headed for. In fact I am in heaven with a lot of wonderful people," I began.

It was getting late and Edwin noticed that no one else was bolting for the door and began to have some hope. Maybe this could go somewhere, although he was not sure about this whole adventure himself.

Jackie, the Spiritualist, slowly began sharing, "Enrique, Barbara, Jill, Mike, Ben, we just met tonight and I am so glad to have met you. You don't know how Edwin and I know each other. I am part of the Spiritualist movement. We both belong to the Spiritualist Church of Two Worlds in San Leandro. Spiritualist churches are often led by a medium and during the service they may have readings, connecting someone in the congregation with someone in the spirit world." Jackie was a calming presence you could feel safe with

"I was an assistant pastor to an evangelical church in Fremont for many years, that is, until I started having some very clear dreams of my daughter who died twenty years ago when she was only three." Jackie choked up a little and her eyes were beginning to fill with tears. "She is a very strong and beautiful woman in heaven now. It is not evil to connect to those who have passed on. It is very real and very wonderful."

Jill, who had been silent since she fainted, had tears in her eyes. "I know it is real, but I was afraid. My son also died, ten years ago, in a car crash. I... I guess he was drunk and it was after the senior prom. His name was Jerry, and, well, you know, I thought he might be in hell. He was always a little wild."

I had waited for this exchange and knew this was the right time.

"We have three beautiful people with us and I would like them to say some things."

Shirley Jackson, Edwin's mother, began,

"Hello everyone. I am Shirley Jackson, Ed's mom. I am so proud of Edwin for being a part of this and helping these fine people make this connection to you on Earth."

Edwin cautiously smiled with eyebrows raised "That's definitely my Mom."

Next another woman's voice came through,

"Mom. Mom, can you hear me, this is Diane. This is amazing!"

Jackie sobbed, "Diane! Is that you? Oh, baby, I love you so much. Oh my God!"

"I know Mom that is what has carried me all these years. I have so much to tell you but we will talk later."

Finally I said, "We have one more. And yes, he was a little wild, but he is better now."

"Mom? Mom, can you hear me. It's me, Jerry. I know I screwed up, sorry for all the pain I caused you. Please forgive me. I am so sorry."

"Jerry!" Jill screamed, and we all lost it then. Now everyone was crying on both sides of existence.

Mike, who was always a little irreverent, said, "This is cool. I'm in." Ben, who was back to his normal color, said, "Yea, OK, I'm in also."

Chapter 5
Visual Success

Opening Visual Communication

We began to have regular meetings, and I would send out a thought to those involved on our side when the group on the Earthly side was together and ready to begin. In the spirit world, like communication, travel is done by the power of thought. You wish to be somewhere and you are instantly there. But we also have some recognized practices. It is not considered polite to appear directly in someone's home, but rather we materialize on the walkway outside his or her home and then come to the door and knock. If you wish to meet with someone, think of the person, and if he or she lets you know it is a convenient time the person will be there or you can go to them at the speed of thought.

The audio transmission to Earth was cleared up after a few weeks, and actually the group had grown, as those who were at the Thanksgiving gathering had told their friends and family. Who could keep this to themselves? We were happy with the growth, as we certainly had nothing to hide; in fact, we wanted the whole world to know. It was also miraculous to see the changes in these people's lives. They were more confident, more hopeful, more sincere, all around better people. That gave us great hope that this was something very necessary for the world.

Now there were some teenagers showing up at Edwin's house, like Ben's son, Patrick, from a previous marriage. Patrick looked a lot like his dad, short with the dark curly hair, but no glasses. The kid was a genius with everything electronic. It was actually Patrick who came up with the solution to the distortion with the sound. But, like I said, I am not a scientist so don't ask me to explain.

Surprisingly Edwin's house had become a hangout for these young people, even when Edwin wasn't there. Edwin was secretly proud of this. Patrick brought in some of his friends and soon Edwin's house would not be big enough for everyone. Making videos, video phone calls and video conferencing was something that everyone in modern society was familiar with, but setting up a video conference between the spirit world and the physical world was a whole new challenge. It was, in fact, the ubiquitous video taping and then posting on social media sites done by everyone, especially the youth, that brought our friends on Earth into their first public challenge, but I will go into all that later. (You can see by my writing that I have had to educate myself about a lot of modern technology, activities and phrases to be able to write all this.)

Also, many of the people joining the group wanted to speak with someone who had passed, but we didn't want to get sidetracked from our main task and asked everyone to be patient. Not only that, but after searching for and finding some of the people they wanted to talk to, we found that not all were in great places in the spirit world. It was not time to go there yet.

Out of the multiple levels in the spirit world only about six of them would be considered at a level that we would let communication happen. Some of the darkest levels are way too frightening to even consider showing to the world at least in the beginning. All of us in these realms are very familiar with the darker levels as we go there sometimes, disguised as similar hideous spirits yet looking for people who are ready to take responsibility for their crimes against their own lives and their fellow man. Once we find someone who is beginning to take some responsibility for the lives they led, they can be pulled from the realm they are in and begin the slow process of healing and growth. We can see a person in hell finally having a more positive thought as an actual light or glow around their head. It is through this process of helping those most unfortunate wretches and also in helping people on Earth make the right decisions that we also grow and are able to rise after some time and a lot of effort, to higher levels.

Jerry, Jill's son, was in a very dark hopeless level but he has grown so much since we first found him. For some, it is better that they do die young as their life direction could have led to great pain to themselves and others. For others who die innocent at a young age, this brings great suffering to their family and friends, some who then even blame God for their loss. There is no simple answer to how and when a person dies, everyone has free will to decide what to do moment to moment along with the overall direction of his or her life. But it is from our great ignorance that we fear death and look at it as a devastating event.

For those of us in the spirit world we know that death is just our second birth, a time of transition, a new beginning to our eternal lives. It is certainly not to be feared, especially for those who have lived lives with some love, some goodness, some care for others. This birth should be a time of celebrating the person's life on Earth with the promise to see them after our own passing.

We knew Jill, Jerry's mom, would be very important to our initial outreach to Edwin's friends so we felt very urgent to find and help Jerry.

We were surprised to find out how important Jerry would be to our work, as he soon became friends with Patrick on Earth and many of Patrick's friends and he shared on a very personal level all that he had gone through and the lessons learned. We could see a real transformation in the heart of many of these young people. I was in the studio when I overheard Jerry explaining to the young people about what had happened in his life and after life.

"In today's world it is very cool to be gangster, to listen to gangster rap and be a bad ass," Jerry was saying. "I was a real shit, disrespecting my mom and everyone else. It's amazing I even graduated from high school. At prom night my girl and I were drinking orange juice we secretly spiked with vodka and were getting trashed. We hopped in my car and drove to go to another party. I hit another car that had a nice family in it and we both went into a spin. The parents and one of their children died in that accident. I'm responsible for that." The kids listening could hear Jerry pause with a heavy catch in his throat.

"My car flipped and I guess I broke my neck. Suddenly I was outside the car looking at this wreck and didn't know what was going on. I could see the hand of my girlfriend sticking out of the shattered window on her side of the car. I called her name but got no response, but I guess she lived through that. Suddenly I was surrounded by some nasty looking people who started beating me and dragged me away. I was yelling and screaming and they were just laughing at me, saying I will get what I deserve now."

"It took me a long time to realize that I was dead. People kept saying I was in hell with them and to stop whining. I was in a dark, dark place that smelled like rotting flesh. It was cold and damp and people were always starting fights, biting and hitting each other. I felt I needed to join a gang to survive. I'm sorry to tell you this, to frighten you with my story. But being a gangster is not cool and to die full of hate is horrible. And now look, my tattoos are gone, I'm so glad. They were some nasty ass tattoos. I still have to take responsibility for that family." All these teenagers were listening to this exchange with their eyes wide open, taking it all in.

Both Martha and I had the feeling that Jerry could be a great help reaching our own son, Samuel.

It was this once tragic young man, Jerry working with Patrick and all these young people that a solution to the video transfer from the spirit world to the physical was breached. Again I am not an engineer, but with relentless tinkering on both sides Patrick and Jerry were trying to get an image of a beautiful bird, native only in the spirit world, to show up on Patrick's iPhone. Jerry was constantly adjusting his spirit side camera set to an extremely low frequency, when Patrick suggested they work with waves instead of direct flow. Jerry went to the spirit world scientists and they worked on this as a possibility, since radio waves were the reason for much of the communication technology successes.

It was a foggy April 15, 2021 when the group at Edwin's house heard a dog bark and a very blurred and pixilated picture of a black dog showed up on the separate dedicated computer. Edwin had bought a separate dedicated Apple computer for this work that was on all the time in case some image came through. Patrick's girlfriend, Elsa, looked over and said that looks like her dog, Shambles, who died in January and she began making a video with her phone of what was happening on the computer monitor.

It was, in fact, Shambles who showed up at my door about three months ago and we knew this dog had belonged to one of the families on Earth that we were involved with. Shambles, a beautiful black Labrador/mix, had lived to a good dog age of twelve years old and was a loyal and happy dog. In the later years Shambles had lost a lot of hair on his back and was partially lame after he was hit by a car that mangled his back left leg. Now in the spirit world he was full of energy, young and beautiful again.

Animals that are loved on Earth become resurrected in the spirit world and often are there to greet their human family members when they pass over along with the human spirits who want to be there for the passing.

We often fail to realize the power we were given, as God intended us to be His sons and daughters and therefore co-creators with Him. The power of our thought, the power of our love and the power of other strong emotions, some good, some destructive are tools we use in creating our own environment. Apparently, scientists on Earth are just beginning to discover the strength of human thought, even to the point that there is no such thing as an objective observer. Experiments can go one way or in an entirely different direction based on who is observing the experiment. In the case of Shambles and so many other animals now living in the spirit world, by human love we are given the awesome power to give eternal life to animals we cherish.

All the adults were at work, but the kids had the day off from school celebrating spring break and were around the house chatting, laughing, and some of the boys were playing "Chaos Theory IV" or some such computer game. The teens rushed over to the computer monitor and then they saw a hand reach down and pat the dog. The face of a young handsome black man came on the screen and they heard, "Hi, I'm Jerry." Shambles looked up and licked his face and barked again.

Everyone was up on their feet, jumping and yelling. "Oh my God!" "We've done it." "Oh, wow."

"And yes, Elsa, this is Shambles." Jerry said, laughing.

Patrick texted his Dad, Ben, at Micro Sun International, "We have video!"

Elsa's video of this first encounter, video and audio, of life in spirit world was posted on her Facebook page with the heading "My Dog is Alive Again!" She immediately got many responses from friends who were not part of the group and she naively explained that she was part of a group that was connecting to people who have died. The video and her response went viral.

Although we were not ready to expose this to the world, we who had been in the spirit world long before all this modern communication technology was even imagined were the naive ones.

Chapter 6
Public Introduction

The Beginning

The scientists and engineers from both sides began to work on the images until they were clear and distinct. Two well-known scientists, both of whom had made great progress in both audio and visual work around the beginning of the twentieth century, became very interested in our work and with their input we made quicker progress. Thomas Edison and Nikola Tesla, both famous inventors at the end of the nineteenth century to the middle of the twentieth century, who had worked together while on Earth though not always amicably, were just the people to push over the last technical hurdles. It was Edison and Tesla working with Jerry, who was a quick learner that together made the breakthrough on April 15th.

Although we were not quite ready for the world, the world was ready for us, or at least the headline seeking tabloid television shows were. We quickly decided that Elsa, as a young teenager who had inadvertently started the exposure, could obviously not be our public spokesperson.

But I looked at Patrick and Elsa and felt they would have a very important part to play in the near future. Elsa was a very cute chatty brunette with freckles and wide eyes. She adored Patrick.

The Earth group decided on Edwin, the original host of the Thanksgiving gathering and Jackie, his spiritualist friend, would together represent us, as calls began to come in looking for someone in our group to appear on day and nighttime splash shows. They also decided they needed a name, and did not want to use the spirit side name, Jiva Satata, as that was too obscure. Besides, the only people who spoke Sanskrit as their first language had been alive 3,500 years ago or so in ancient India.

They chose the name "New Shambles," in honor of the first living being, Shambles, Elsa's dog, to be shown from the spirit world by computer. They decided they needed a lawyer who could deal with international challenges and to become a corporation, as they may need protection from those who don't like the idea of open communication with the dead. What is the saying, "Dead men tell no tales?" What if dead men can now tell tales and not everyone is comfortable with that. They certainly knew things were going to start happening quickly, but also that this was much bigger than their group and would soon be out of their hands.

In fact, it would be in our hands and we were being guided by some very good and ancient people, some were among the first followers of Jesus, some were ancient Hindu sages, some were early followers of Siddhartha Gautama, the first Buddha, and above them were the founders of these religions themselves now unified in their love for the one and same God. If the Earth was surprised by open communication from the dead wait until they find out who is on the central committee. The scientists and engineers on both sides had done their work and better than expected, but now it was time for another side of Jiva Satata to emerge.

New Shambles became New Shambles, Inc. on June 1, 2021. They contracted a promotion company and this company found their first opportunity.

On June 15th, Edwin and Jackie had their first interview with the new talk show host, Tammy McNeal, in her office. Tammy, blond and short, was vivacious, beautiful and confident, a firecracker. Other established syndicated shows did not want to be the first to open this Pandora's box and the crazies who would flock to it. But Tammy was new, adventurous and needed to start with a loud bang to be able to compete with the popular shows. She recently had some success with a medium that took some calls and also did readings of the dearly departed from among those in her live audience. This seemed like a natural progression in the dealing with the dead business. They set the date for one month on July 15th to have their first live show. Once the deal was set there was heavy promotion on TV, newspapers, and online ads especially using Elsa's video of Jerry and Shambles.

The Tammy Show would be the real launch for New Shambles and Tammy had no idea what she was in for and having a smaller budget than the behemoths she was competing against. Edwin and Jackie, just two regular people in the modern era, knew they were jumping off a cliff with this and that their lives would never be simple again. But, bless them; they were ready to plunge into the abyss anyway. For them it had become a mission. We knew we had found the right people to begin this cataclysmic hurricane about to hit the Earth.

For Jiva Satata we had some very delicate decisions to make. Who would be the first person the world would see and what else would be in this hour introduction to a world not everyone believed in. We thought about having a famous person, like Abraham Lincoln or Mohandas Gandhi, but decided people would feel it was a hoax created before the show with an impersonator pretending to be one of these great men. We also did not want a polarizing person, and anyone famous could fit that description.

So it was decided that my wife, Martha, and I would be the main speakers. After initially introducing ourselves we would first of all explain why this was happening at this time, what our whole motive is. We would describe our life on Earth and also what our life in the spirit world has been like. But more important than us just talking we would show them the realm we live in. Unfortunately there are colors in the spirit world that are not in the physical world and also the vibrancy of the colors can't translate through the computers.

But there certainly were many things we could show, animals that are unique to the spirit world, buildings here, how people travel, maybe even a few minutes with a musical performance. We would interact with the host and with Edwin and Jackie, but not with the audience for this first show. It would be too chaotic and there would not be enough time. Edwin and Jackie were made aware of these plans.

The Tammy Show

On July 15, 2021, there was a marine layer of fog covering the bay area that persisted through the day. Jackie and Edwin arrived at 4 p.m., three hours before the show would start at 7 p.m., as they had been asked to do. They needed to familiarize themselves with the stage and auditorium, be shown from what direction to enter the stage, how to face the audience, to see the big screen that would be used, get prepped with make-up and most importantly to meet Tammy before to build a compatible chemistry together. Tammy was a energetic woman who exuded enthusiasm. She took the whole concept of someone appearing on the screen that was actually long dead in stride.

Perhaps Tammy was unaware that as Jackie and Edwin drove up to the studio there were some groups outside with signs, saying such things as, "Keep Devil Worship Out of America!" and "God Hates Liars!" and another group shouting, "Frauds! Another carnival show!" and a smaller group singing hymns. Well, the circus was just beginning. There was also a long line of people hoping to be admitted in an hour when the doors opened for the audience.

Edwin asked her to make sure the computer that would project onto the screen was not connected to the Internet and to show that to the audience. A technician assisting Tammy said that with wireless technology that would be hard to prove, as a server and router could be anywhere close and yet hidden. OK, but he wanted to know if there was any way to show everyone watching that this was not being transmitted from a remote location. Well, they could set up a blocking device and show how the Internet could no longer be accessed. Jackie said that would be too distracting and that some people would believe this was real and some would not, no matter what.

Edwin had one more preliminary request. They brought along three photographs on a flash drive and would like the photos projected on the secondary screen when prompted. The technician took the flash drive, saying, "Yea, sure, no problem."

Jackie Nagorski had worked hard to be accepted into a male-dominated seminary for the Evangelical Church of America. When she was later assigned as the Assistant Pastor to the Evangelical Free Church in Fremont, California she felt her life purpose was being revealed. She was a great extemporaneous speaker, employing wit and humor in a way that made you feel embraced by the message. But with her experiences with her daughter in spirit world she left the ministry. She found and connected with the Spiritualist Church of the Two Worlds and here she employed her oratory skills, but this time as a lay member who would give introductory talks about interaction with the other side. Jackie volunteered to give the introduction to New Shambles, Inc. and the work they were doing on The Tammy Show. Edwin was completely supportive of the idea, as public speaking was a daunting challenge. He would much rather be the sidekick in this exchange, but he would be willing to supply an explanation of the engineering obstacles they had to overcome, if needed.

With the show beginning, Tammy was on stage welcoming her overflow crowd by blowing kisses to all and saying, "I love you, I love you. Welcome my friends, to The Tammy Show!"

"Tonight we have an amazing show for you, as you must have heard, as I see there is standing room only. Apparently there are many more outside hoping one of you will go to the restroom so they can come in and grab your seat." Laughter erupted.

A man near the back stood up and shouted, "Tammy, why put on this sham? You know they are just scammers, right?"

"Well, sir, I think I remember you when we had the medium here. I am surprised you came back. You must enjoy the shams we put on." Tammy replied. The audience had a good laugh. Someone said, "Sit down and give these people a chance."

"And with that, let's get started. Please let me introduce Edwin Jackson and Jackie Nagorski who are the founders of New Shambles, Inc., an organization that is working to connect your computer and mine to the world of ghosts." Tammy proclaimed.

Edwin and Jackie walked out to center stage, with Jackie leading, striding over to shake Tammy's hand with Edwin right behind. "Please be seated, and welcome to the Tammy Show. Tell us how you came up with this idea of having a séance video conference and why you named your organization, New Shambles. Is this a prediction of what the world will be like after you unleash your horde of undead on us?" asked Tammy smiling.

Edwin cleared his throat and nervously began, "Jackie is a much better speaker, but let me share how this started. First of all, contacting those who have passed on was the last thing on my mind. This was not my idea, it was their idea."

"Whose idea, your great, great grandfather's?" asked Tammy. A chuckle went through the audience.

"No, no some scientist who worked with Napoleon, he said there were a group of scientists and engineers who are in the spirit world who wanted to open up communication with us living on Earth. It was some voice coming though my computer speakers. This happened last October. And then they brought my Mom on, who died June 2019, and she said some things, and I knew it was her."

With that disastrous beginning, Jackie rescued Edwin, took the microphone and began, "Many people believe in life after death, let me ask, who here believes in an eternal life?" Jackie was good, already working the crowd. About 75% of the people in the audience raised their hands.

"If everyone who once lived on Earth, including all those brilliant inventors and scientists and Edwin's great, great grandfather, were now living in a different dimension don't you think some would try to reach us on Earth? I know I sure wouldn't want to sit around all the time singing hymns and playing a harp. Who wants a heaven like that? Yuk."

A relieved laugh rode through the crowd, maybe because Edwin wasn't speaking anymore.

Jackie got serious, "Edwin heard his mom, and another friend heard her son Jerry, who had died in a car crash after senior prom. And I heard my daughter who died twenty years ago when she was three and she is a strong young woman now. Jackie had tears in her eyes. "We got our personal proof and then we got serious and started helping with this amazing experiment." Some of the more tender hearted in the audience had eyes beginning to water also.

Jackie continued, "How many of you saw the video that went viral first with the dog and then the young man coming on camera saying he was from the spirit world?" Almost everyone's hand went up. "Yea, I guess that is why you are all here." An acknowledging laugh burst out. "The audio was the first step and then it took several months with engineers and scientists working on both sides of life to finally break through with the video. The dog you saw was named Shambles and the young man was Jerry. We named our group after the first living being to come through, the dog, Shambles."

Tammy was sitting there with her mouth open, and then realizing that she closed it quickly and said, "OK, well what do you have for us today?"

Edwin made a motion to the technician he had given the flash drive to and three pictures came on the smaller screen, one of a young black puppy with white feet and another of the same dog but old, with gray hairs around his muzzle and losing hair on his back, his left leg bent at a bad angle, and finally a picture of an African-American high school boy with a cocky smile who looked like a young delinquent.

Jackie said, "This, as you probably have guessed is Shambles as a pup, the next picture a month before Shambles died, and the young man is Jerry. And if our friends on the other side are ready, let the show begin."

There was a loud bark and then a man's voice said, "Good boy, Shambles." The large central screen came to life and there was a man, who looked like an older version of the young Jerry and with him a dog that looked like, not an old dying black Labrador/mix with white feet, but a young vibrant dog full of energy with his tail wagging his whole backside. "Hi everyone, I'm Jerry Tanner, and this is my good friend, Shambles."

The heckler from the back jumped up and yelled, "Bogus! You're probably in a back studio! What a scam!"

Tammy knew there was no back studio, and that the screen was connected to their computer system only, and did not have a way to receive a wireless transmission. Many people in the audience had pulled out their smart phones and were Googling Jerry Tanner. Most of the studios don't allow phones on while taping, but Tammy felt it was all right as long as everyone's phone was silent. No one was allowed to make or receive calls, but Tammy was fine with anyone who wanted to make videos while the show was in progress and then to post it on social sites. It might bring a lot more people to start watching the show, and today a flood of new people were connecting. There were quite a few people holding up their phones making videos and others who were Instagraming, texting and tweeting.

Jerry continued, "I was a young punk who ten years ago thought the world owed me. I was so full of myself. I didn't care about anyone else, and then when I had the car accident, I…, well I died. I don't want to freak you out but for many years I was in a dark place surrounded by selfish destructive people, just like me. But I am not the main show today. I owe everything to this couple who came down to where I was in hell and began sharing about a much better place, and that if I could begin to take responsibility for what I had done and to help others I could grow step by step, to better and better levels. I would like to introduce a couple I love with all my heart. They saved my life. This is…"

Before Jerry could introduce my wife and me, a elder woman stood up and called out, "What about Jesus? No one has said anything about believing in Jesus as your Lord and Savior." Several people proclaimed their agreement. "Once you go to hell, you are there for eternity," a red faced man declared, "There is no get out of jail card by doing good deeds after you die." Some people got up and walked out of the studio, and as they did another woman turned and shot back, "This is evil, don't listen to this trickery, or this demon will bring you all to hell with him." Some people who had been on the sides moved in to take the vacated seats.

Jerry fumbled, "No, it's not like that. Wait! The couple that helped me are Christians, I think. They talk about God all the time."

Tammy had to consider whether to wrap this up or see where it would go. She did find it fascinating and was just starting to believe this was real, plus she still had thirty five minutes of the show to fill. But it was Jackie who stood up and waving her arms, shouted, "Hello everybody! For those who are still here, please give us a chance. Please listen to the next couple. Dan and Martha are you there?"

Jerry moved away from the camera with Shambles bounding after him. In our living room is spirit world, I moved to the chairs set up for us, pulled the seat out for Martha and she sat next to my chair, then I sat down. We were dressed in comfortable clothes, not from colonial America as we felt that would look like we were wearing costumes to fool people. I had on nice slacks and a button shirt and Martha was wearing a very nice flowing dress with large floral designs of many colors.

Jackie looked at Tammy, "Are we OK, can we continue?"

Tammy smiled, nodded and said, "Yes, please. You're giving me one hell of a show, or one heaven of a show, or something like that."

Jackie looked at the crowd and said, "I would like you to meet Daniel and Martha Everheart, who lived in Colonial America before the American Revolution."

There was a collective gasp and everyone was fully attentive. There was still a good-sized audience left, this being California and not the Bible belt, but people didn't know how to welcome this couple, some clapped. A man called out, "Hello ghostly people." Everyone laughed and the tension was broken.

Martha began after a short laugh, "We know this is very sensitive and a lot of people won't believe this is happening at first. There is a lot of confusion on Earth now and people have very strong beliefs, as we saw earlier. But the time has come for the walls between the Earth and what we call the spirit lands or the spirit world to be removed. We did not decide this, nor did a group of scientists, this is a direction from our loving God. It is time."

She continued, "We are not here to debate theology, because that also will have little meaning as this progresses. This is much bigger than a television show, although I do want to thank our host, Tammy McNeal, for opening up this platform to us. But folks your world is about the change."

A great applause went up for Tammy and she nodded with a smile, although inside she was overwhelmed.

I spoke up, "Yes, we are very grateful, Tammy. Thank you. Very soon there will be shows all over the world with different speakers from the spirit side who speak the local language and who come from the local customs and religions. I am not a scientist, engineer or inventor and I have had to do a lot of catching up to see how the Earth has progressed with cars, airplanes, computers, phones, the internet. Believe me, these were not in the world we lived in. We had horses, wooden carts, and everything was one of a kind made by hand, even the clothes we wore. We did not have spare time for anything beyond our daily work. And for this opportunity to greet you we didn't want to dress as we did on Earth 250 years ago because that would have been pretentious since we don't dress that way here anymore."

I continued, "Why is this happening now? Mankind has been growing spiritually for thousands of years with an escalation in the last 150 years. Also technological innovation has mushroomed to the point now where each person in an audience can be making a video of a video conference from the spirit world, post it on a social site, where anyone in the world can view the video that was just posted say 5,000 miles away and comment on it, and the comments can also be seen by anyone in the world, all instantaneously. With me speaking like this, I know I don't sound like someone who lived before electricity was even discovered. What you don't realize on Earth is that the physical world is becoming more and more like the spirit world, with instant communication, air travel, video phones that can reach anyone in the world. Now is clearly the time for the walls to be removed between the two sides of life."

Tammy, wanting to still be relevant on her own show asked, "Mr. and Mrs. Everheart, how do we know that you actually are from this spirit world? You sound very much like a modern couple although you do have an accent I can't quite place."

Martha responded, "This one show will not convince most people that communication has now opened up between the two worlds. As we said earlier, this is just the beginning. But we would like to show you a little of our world. Would you like that?"

Tammy smiled and addressed her audience, "What do think? Do you want to see what heaven looks like?"

A great roar went up from the crowd, "Yes!", "Wow!", "Is this real?" and, of course, "I still say they are probably in a back studio," came from the back.

We stood up and Martha said, "This is not the highest heaven, it is our home and we love it every day. There are colors here that you don't have so the technology will translate it to the closest possible colors. We have been sitting in our home during this conference, so let's go out our front door and look around."

Cameras had been set up before the conference and the view shifted to these outside. The audience then saw on the screen the beautiful view from our home, the flowing hills with a profusion of flowers of vibrant, harmonizing colors all around. Our many fruit trees were close to our home each surrounded by more flowers. Many of the flowers and trees were unique to the spirit lands, not found on Earth. The air was crystal clear, as always with the constant warming sun magnifying the beauty. A large bird with magnificent plumage landed near us; and one of the cameras focused on it. She spread her wings and a couple more birds, just as beautiful, but of a different species also landed nearby. None of these types of birds could be found on Earth.

Shambles, who had been running around outside, came up to the birds and the birds and dog had great fun with each other, and one even landed on Shambles back and he ran around barking happily with his welcome passenger flapping it's wings to stay on.

Not a sound came from the studio audience and many sat with their mouths open.

I held out my hand and a couple bees landed on it, danced around and then buzzed off in delight with so many flowers to choose from.

My wife and I laughed, and I said, "Everyday here is a delight and special. If you don't mind, we want to take you into town in the last few moments that we have for this show."

Instantly the view changed and we were in the middle of a beautiful town bustling with happy people everywhere.

There was a gasp from the audience.

I said, "Sorry we had no time to explain how things work here. Travel is done by thought, it is instantaneous, and because we were of one mind we all came here together."

Constantly the people in the town were in flux with some of the people in the town disappearing and others appearing, but there was laughter everywhere, people hugging each other or walking arm in arm. Some golden shimmering butterflies were darting joyfully in and out through the crowd. An incandescent hummingbird with long tail feathers hovered near the camera and then flitted away. Martha pointed to a magnificent building with a golden dome, "This building here is the Hall of Art, and in there you will find thousands of master works, not the ones painted on the Earth but the real originals that were first in the mind of the artist who made them."

"We have plays, theater, orchestras, all types of music, all arts and crafts, halls of inventions, halls of learning, all things that bring joy to people. You can learn skills that you always wanted to learn, meet people who lived at any time on the Earth and travel to your heart's content, even around the galaxy and the whole universe." Martha added.

There were a few people on a nearby corner, one woman with a guitar, a man with a flute like instrument and together with others singing a folksy song, unknown on Earth. As they were singing, beautiful colors were swirling above their heads almost like a dance accompanying their beautiful song.

The show's technician was waving at Tammy, pointing to his wrist as if he had a watch there and she was shocked to see that the time had gotten away from them, exclaimed, "I'm so sorry but we need to bring this show to a close."

There was a moan of protest from the studio. Tammy said, "Daniel or Martha, do you have any parting words for us?"

Martha said, "Yes, don't live your life with the aim to go to heaven, live your life with love for all people, help others and pray for others, friends and strangers and give thanks to God every day for the gift of being alive. This is just the beginning of the transformation and you are the most fortunate people to ever live, to be able to witness this time."

Tammy pleaded, "Will you come back to my show?"

I put my arm around Martha and said, "We would love to, thank you Tammy."

The big screen gave a little pop and the image shrank down to a light in the center and then it was gone.

Many people were crying, many were standing, staring with open mouths; others were sitting there with a scowl on their face, arms folded over their chest. The heckler's voice came, closer to the stage this time, "Wow, did you hire Spielberg to create this? That was well done."

Tammy had tears in her eyes and said, "I don't have the budget to do something like that. Oh my, oh my." Regaining her composure she said, "Thank you Edwin and Jackie and thank you everyone for coming to the Tammy Show."

And everyone, except those who were still in shock, jumped to their feet and gave her a thunderous standing ovation.

The Aftermath

Within a day it seemed that everyone everywhere knew about what had happened on the Tammy Show and everyone had an opinion. Snippets of the show, especially of the shots outside our home and in the town were constantly being played on News programs with headlines such as; "Is this really heaven?" or "Can this be real?" There were also shots of the Christians who had left angry, denouncing the show as demonic along with Martha saying that differences in theology would have little meaning soon. Most startling was the proclamation that these types of visitations would soon be happening all over the world with hosts of different religions and cultures.

The headline the next day for the Oakland Tribune said, "Did We Just See Heaven?" with the story detailing what had transpired on the show. Their question was the same we had asked ourselves in planning this first show, "Why didn't some famous person from history come on the show, someone everyone would recognize?"

The Southern Baptist headquarters in Nashville, Tennessee declared this as a sign of the anti-Christ and that whoever believed or participated in these video aberrations received a mark on their forehead, destined for eternal hell. The Cardinal of the Los Angeles region of the Roman Catholic Church, who had made great effort in ecumenical outreach, felt this was an attack on the Christian church in general since Martha did not talk about Jesus and had said that different religious people, from heaven no less, would be hosting these shows. "How could Hindus, with their belief in millions of gods, ever go to heaven?" he had asked. "Are they going to confirm to the people in India that God is a blue god?" he continued, referring to Krishna.

A reporter for Rai News 24, an Italian state owned TV station, asked a representative for the Vatican what the Pope thought about the revelations from the Tammy Show. He was told that the Pope was concerned that this "heaven" revealed in the show was not consistent with the scriptures, but would have no official comment at this time.

Richard Fish, the Leader of the American Atheists representing 50,000 members, went on The Morning Show demanding an official inquiry into New Shambles, Inc. and to find out which special effects company was behind this fraud. He felt that the host, Tammy, was just as ambushed by the contents of the show as the American people were.

The Imam of Iran, representing Shia Muslims and an Imam in Saudia Arabia of the Sunni branch both declared what was expressed in the Tammy Show as another attempt by satanic America to destroy the faith of true believers of Allah. A crowd in Palestine burned in effigy a dummy representing Tammy along with the American flag while chanting, "Death to the infidels!"

Throughout the world there were news clips of people protesting with signs about "the lies" from the Tammy Show. All over America people on street corners were assembled holding up signs that said, "My heaven is full of people who love Jesus" or "Honk if you believe in Jesus, not other gods!" or "That was not my heaven!"

Well if one brief show about the spirit world could produce this much reaction we were eager to move to the next phase.

Chapter 7
The India Show

Garuda and Rajinda

We met Garuda and Rajinda earlier at the celebration in the spirit world. Now let me introduce them more thoroughly. In our organization, Jiva Satata, there were people from all religions still represented on Earth along with many spirits who had believed in ancient, now extinct religions. Not everyone had lived lives of goodness and love, and many who now live in the higher realms had been brutal and merciless to those around them while on Earth. That they were now in the realms of light meant they had overcome enormous obstacles to advance this far.

Over 5,000 years ago, Jéagugun lived in what is now known as the Karnataka Rain Forest in southern India. His name meant "The Terrible One" and he led his tribe in many ruthless battles against neighboring tribes. If they captured any enemy warriors or took any captives from the village they would allow the women to slowly torture them with fire and mutilation over many days and finally slice them open, capturing the blood. This blood was given to all the tribe to drink as a celebration of their victory. When Jéagugun was around 35 years old a younger warrior betrayed him and stabbed him in the back so he could become the new chief.

Jéagugun had been a cannibal tribal leader and when killed he went to a hell that was full of cannibals attacking and killing their victims, each other. Of course since no one could die again the victims would revive bloody and disfigured and attack others in an endless cycle. They attacked with their fists, fingernails and teeth ripping and tearing. They had no weapons since they had not earned the right to create anything by the power of thought. The battlegrounds were barren fields with pools of filthy tar and fires all around, the sky was black with swirling black clouds and an ever present lightning storm. Many of the people in this level would slink around in their hideous disfigured forms looking for someone else to attack or join in one of the larger battles so they could mangle many people at one time.

It is God's love that provides the light in the spirit world and for those who share no relationship with the goodness of God they live in a most hideous place. In the blackest hell none of God's love can reach the people, since the environment is a product of the wretched people themselves, by their hate, anger and repulsive thoughts.

For over a thousand years Jéagugun lived in this blackest hell, knowing and experiencing no love, no forgiveness, no mercy, only the vilest warfare. One day after an especially horrible battle, he lay bleeding and he felt so tired and thought, "Is there anything else?" At that moment there happened to be some Hindu followers who had come down to this wretched foul smelling place, disguised as other lost souls, to find someone who might be ready to begin growth.

The Hindus saw a hideous figure huddled on the ground, bleeding and groaning. A repulsive smell, of rotting burnt flesh, of excrement, of all things vile filled this place gaging the throat and clogging the pores. It was freezing cold and pitch black as none of God's love could reach those who had never cared for anyone but themselves. Rajinda, one of the women, could see a slight glow above the head of this unfortunate man. She was drawn to him because this light above his head meant he was beginning to be sorry for his life. She knelt to him and said, "Good sir, can I help you?"

"I have never been a good sir, lady, and why are you in this hell? What did you do to deserve this?" Jéagugun responded in anger.

"I am here to find you and to help you," Rajinda said. "Please tell me about your life. Do you have any regrets?"

"What do you mean you are here to help me? No one has cared for me for hundreds of years, not my wife, not my children, no one in my tribe. Who are you then and why would you care for me?" Jéagugun asked indignant. He could feel Rajinda's concern for him and it was beginning to penetrate his defenses.

"I come from a different place than this, a place that is not dark, there is some light and good people. I came here to find you and to give you a chance to change your life. Do you want that?" Rajinda asked and a warm glow was surrounding her. Rajinda's smile was warm and sweet the first Jéagugun saw for a thousand years. She was short at around five foot, three inches and beautiful.

"What do I have to do to go to this place? I will do anything to leave this horrid place," Jéagugun said and reached his bony clawed hand towards her. His skin was rancid with boils and open soars. Rajinda did not recoil from this apparition, but reached out and held his hand and prayed to Krishna to help this lost soul. "Lord Krishna, please help our brother here. He has suffered for hundreds of years and now is ready to begin to grow. We are here to help him have some light in his soul. Bless him with hope and understanding. Thank you."

Very slowly over many days she gained his trust and over what would be many years helped him to understand there were other choices. From so very long ago, he remembered that his mother had loved him, and this woman reminded him of her, and he thanked her. That one act of appreciation was enough for him to rise to the next level of hell. This Hindu woman, Rajinda, and her friends were tenacious and extremely patient believing that to help others would also help their own karma.

After several hundred years after meeting Rajinda, Jéagugun had risen to a gray level and had many times organized his own groups to go back into hell to find other deplorable creatures that were ready to be helped. With Rajinda's help he was rising more quickly and in the next hundred years was in realms that are considered the first of the heavenly levels and now was helping Rajinda in her growth. In this realm he changed his name to Garuda, which is Sanskrit for celestial bird or white-crested eagle and is one of the Hindu gods. In the more modern era, Garuda and Rajinda, forever companions, were some of the founders of Jiva Satata. Their love for each other and for God was incredible. We all felt so blessed when they would visit our realm. Together, Garuda and Rajinda, wanted to host a show in India, especially to reach out to the Hindi religion.

Outreach to India

Although not the original intent, India, China, Southeast Asia, Africa, Mexico, South America and other developing countries have all benefited greatly from American and other developed nations whose companies outsourced much of their workforce to these developing nations. Although this caused a lot trouble back in America, it fit into God's plan. America was blessed not for itself but so it could help the world.

If America would not willingly share its technology and progress, then God would use their desire to make greater profits as a means to spread knowledge and development throughout the world. Whenever a company outsources its workforce to other countries to save money on labor costs they have to train the workers and set up the infrastructure, the plants, the factories, the equipment and the tools. Some workers would have to be trained in each step of the manufacturing process and some were trained to become managers who understood the culture of their fellow workers, as a bridge to the American owners and managers. With that investment some of these managers who worked closely with the American managers become experienced to the point that they can then start their own companies.

Because of outsourcing, hundreds of thousands of young Indians were trained in computers, in software design, a vast array of electronics along with manufacturing all parts needed for all types of gadgets and populating large tech support phone banks. India is also one of the most devotedly religious countries in the world, so it was not hard for Garuda and Rajinda to find young Hindi technical entrepreneurs on Earth and to start reaching out to them through their computers, following the same path that had worked in America with New Shambles. We had already made the breakthrough in video conferencing from the spirit worlds but now we wanted to take it a step further.

Raj and Ileana Kumar were a young couple who worked for the Hewlett-Packard Corporate office in Bangalore, India. Ileana's father, Mr. Maneesh Dasgupta, worked as a producer for C-Bangalore Channel 4 Television. Raj was tall with wavy dark hair and a perpetual 5 o'clock shadow, Illeana was darker and comely in her colorful saris.

One morning while Ileana was sweeping the walkway outside their home, she heard what sounded like her grandmother calling from the house. She went in and saw to her shock and astonishment that it was her grandmother's face on her laptop and when she saw her favorite granddaughter called out her affectionate name for her, "my little rose!" "Nanna!" Ileana gasped, "But you died. Your body was cremated, I still have some of the ashes." "Yes, I know, and it was such a lovely ceremony, and thank you for preparing the garland of roses for me and for the special picture of Ganesha, the one I love." She continued, "And although I appreciated it at the time, you really did not need to have my cremation pyre at the Ganges. That was a great expense for your father."

"But you died, Nanna, how can I be talking to you?" Ileana persisted.

"Oh yes, I guess that is a little disturbing." Mrs. Kashi Dasgupta exclaimed. Apparently dying was not a cure for absentmindedness; Kashi was still Kashi, with the biggest heart but a simpler mind.

Kashi explained, "Well, you see, where I live now a very nice couple approached me and asked if I would mind introducing them to you. They are here with me now, would you like to meet them?"

"Oh Nanna, I love you so much. I am so happy to see you again." Ileana said with tears streaming down her cheeks. "I don't know what is happening, but sure I would like to meet your friends. Will I see you again?"

"Anytime you like, from what I understand. My dear, this is Garuda and Rajinda. They will tell what is happening. I love you too, my little rose," Kashi said with so much love in her eyes.

Next on the screen were Rajinda and Garuda sitting on flat embroidered pillows on a hardwood floor. There was a beautiful batik tapestry of a male and female deer near a mountain stream behind them. An exquisite vase with the most incredible flowers of all colors was on a small table next to Rajinda. Both bowed at their waists with their hands clasped before them in a sign of blessing and respect.

"Hello Ileana, it is our deep pleasure to meet you," Rajinda began. "Do you remember the news stories about a television show in America, called the Tammy Show? Do you remember what that was about?" continued Garuda.

Ileana felt the blood leave her face, "Oh my God, everyone knows about that. Then that really was my grandmother?"

"Yes and she is a wonderful person, such a delight to be around," Rajinda laughed. "My husband and I have been in the spiritual realms for many thousands of years and it is always wonderful to meet new people.

Garuda got to the business at hand, "If you are willing, we would like you and your husband to approach your father to do a show about life in the spirit world on the television station he works for. What do you think about that?"

Ileana noticed there was such a presence around this couple, even through the translation of the camera and computer screen, and her heart beat faster. They didn't have the bindi dot on their forehead, but they definitely looked like they were of Indian descent. When they looked at each other there was so much love flowing through a simple gaze.

"Um, I don't know. I have to go to work now and I would need to talk to my husband. I don't know what my father would say. Let me get back to you on that, but wait, how do I do that?" Ileana stammered. "What am

I saying? This is insane!"

"Don't tell your father this, but tonight he is going to have a very interesting dream and if he is undecided the next night he will have another dream. Your grandmother says he can be quite stubborn. But don't worry he will not be harmed or threatened. We don't work like that," Rajinda declared.

"I understand that you and your husband are not working tomorrow, so we will visit you both tomorrow morning. Fill free to prepare your husband, Raj, I believe his name is," said Rajinda. "And I like his name."

"Nameste and may you be filled with God's love," the couple said together and with hands clasped in front of them bowed at the waist. Their image disappeared and Rajinda's email page that the computer had been opened to before all the transmissions began, was back on the screen.

Rajinda sat at her kitchen table, put her head in her hands and said, "Oh my God, how am I supposed to go to work after that?" And realizing she would be useless at work that day, called in sick.

"Nanna!" she sobbed.

Preparing for the Show in India

Maneesh Dasgupta had worked his way from the go-for man to the go-to man at Channel 4 Television. He was ambitious, stubborn and demanding; not an easy person to be around. His parents, Yamir and Kashi Dasgupta, had both died in July 2012 during a visit to Yamir's hometown of Assam, India when a riot broke out between Bodos (of both Christian and Hindu faith) and Muslims that resulted in 77 deaths. Ileana was nineteen years old at the time her grandparents had died. Her father was then Assistant Manager of the News Department for Channel 4.

When Maneesh was a boy his parents ran a little shop on Narayana Pillai Street in Bangalore selling cameras, film and other photographic supplies along with developing film and making prints. It was 1983 while one of the photographers who worked for a news program on Channel 4 was buying film that he noticed young Maneesh who was running around the store helping customers or going to the back at his father's request to bring out different items. Although only sixteen, the photographer said he could help Maneesh get a job as the person who would run errands for his department. Since he was still a minor, Channel 4 worked out a deal where his father would receive 60% of his earnings until he was eighteen. Yamir agreed to this deal since it brought a new source of income to the family.

With that start Maneesh worked his way up to a photographer's assistant, to a photographer and then into management. In 2019 he became a Producer for Channel 4, with a strong voice on what shows would run.

That night on Friday, August 13, 2021, Maneesh was tired after working for ten hours plus it was during the monsoon rainy season. Today it had started to rain in the afternoon and by the time he headed home it was pouring rain. His wife, Adrika, ran out to the car with an umbrella to escort him to the house. Usually when Maneesh was home he would watch his station, Channel 4, with an obsessive interest. Today he just wanted to enjoy his wife's cooking and watch a Bollywood movie with her. They decided on the 2014 movie, Ankhon Dekhi starring Sanjay Mishra who, after a dramatic incident, decides that he will only believe what he sees with his eyes. They, of course, did not realize that interested parties from the spirit realms influenced their choice of a movie.

Maneesh went to bed around 10:30 while his wife stayed up a little later. His dreams at first were the usual forgettable snippets that bounced here and there. Finally there was a powerful blue light that vibrated with energy. The light seemed to come from high above hitting the ground all around him. A highly decorated boat seemed to float up to him with five ladies in shimmering red saris with golden trim and gold bracelets, anklets, earrings and nose rings. They were holding a canopy and singing a bhajan, a Hindu devotional song of love for the Divine. The lady in the middle looked at him, and said, "Maneesh, you are like Ankhon Dekhi, only believing what you see with your own eyes. Make it happen so many more who are just like you can see and believe." Maneesh responded, "Make what happen?" Once again the lady said, "Make it happen so many more can believe."

The next morning Ileana and Raj had a light breakfast and Raj was working on their desktop computer. At the Hewlett-Packard Corporate Office Raj had developed and maintained the corporate website, showing new products and company developments, getting feedback from customers, both retailers and the public, reporting on Board meetings, along with financial statements for the India branch. Ileana had told

Raj about the computer visitation from Garuda and Rajinda, about her Grandmother speaking to her from beyond the grave and that they said they would visit with them today and explain more of how Raj and Ileana could help them. Raj was a little floored at this and really didn't know how to respond so he took more of a wait-and-see-what-happens approach.

Raj was looking over the corporate website to see how it functioned on anyone's home computer, not logging in as the administrator. This way he could look for bugs or glitches that he might not see as the administrator. He clicked on the link to view the bio pages of the executive staff, when instead of a static picture of his boss, he was looking at another man, and this man was turning his face and looking at him. Raj jerked his head back, and said, "What the...? Who are you?"

The man said, "Hello Raj. I am Garuda, the man from the spirit lands that your wife told you about." Raj quickly checked the source code to see where this was coming from, but the only code he saw was from the corporate page he had been looking at. Cautiously he came back to the video screen, "OK, my wife said she had this incredible experience with her grandmother and with two other people all saying they were from the land of the dead. We saw that YouTube video of that show in America where other people said they were from the same place. It seemed a little contrived to me. But then I don't know how you could imitate Ileana's grandmother. She definitely believes it was her grandmother."

A beautiful lady came over and sat next to Garuda, they both looked to be in their early thirties or late twenties and of Indian heritage. She was wearing an exquisite violet sari that had flower designs in gold thread. Garuda said, "Raj, I would like you to meet my wife, Rajinda. Could you have your wife, Ileana, come here also so we can address you both together?"

"Look, if this is a scam, we are not interested. I don't want my wife to be hurt or be given some false hope." Raj said.

But Ileana was just coming in from their garden and saw who was on the computer screen. Ileana put her hand on her mouth and said, "Oh my God, it's them!"

"Now look, Ileana, we don't know who these people are or what they are up to," stressed Raj.

Rajinda said, "We know it is hard to believe that we are talking to you from the land of spirits. So we want you, Raj, to ask us to show you whatever you would like to see here. We could bring a relative of yours who has passed into this realm, but we want to try another way to show you we are what we say we are. For the billions who will see the shows we can't have everyone's deceased family members come on to convince them. So you name it and we will show you, if possible."

"OK" said Raj, "Show me God."

Garuda and Rajinda both laughed. "Well, that is why we said, if possible. God is a spirit that no one sees, not while living on Earth or in the Spirit Lands. We feel God's love and presence all the time, but nobody sees God. He does not have a form that can be seen."

"Well then," Raj continued, "Show me hell."

The couple became very serious and saddened, but instantly the scene changed to a very gray landscape with brown dead grass and filthy hovels with some deformed people in rags yelling and attacking each other. "This is a lower level, but not by far the blackest hell. They can't see or hear us here. I was a much worse beast than the people you see here when I died. It took thousands of years to grow to the person I am now, and I owe that to my wife. She found me and slowly helped me to take responsibility for all the pain and suffering I had caused. She saved my life, and we got married here in the spirit world," explained Garuda.

Ileana asked, her eyes wide and her mouth open, "What did these people do to end up here?" "The people in this realm were wealthy bankers and business people who only loved their money, they swindled people, destroyed smaller businesses, foreclosed on poor family homes or did whatever they could for a profit," said Rajinda. "We won't show you lower hells, as you would not be able to bare it."

Ileana couldn't take this anymore, and blurted out, "Can you show us a waterfall?"

Instantly Garuda and Rajinda were smiling and holding hands near an incredible waterfall. The crashing water was making beautiful music, not something an orchestra would make, but harmonious soothing sounds. The water below the waterfall was crystal clear with fish of all colors swimming around. There was a small herd of deer nearby, and seeing Garuda and Rajinda hurried over to be petted and loved. There were dazzling flowers around the pool at the bottom of the waterfall and along the river that flowed away.

Raj had watched all this and finally said, "You said you were in hell thousands of years ago. How old are you?"

"We are over 5,000 years old, long before India was a nation, there were just warring tribes. But, Hinduism was believed by some, even then, including Rajinda. I had never heard of Hinduism while I was alive. My tribe were cannibals and very savage. I was a tribal leader until I was murdered," Garuda explained.

"But you look young, in your twenties or thirties," Raj countered.

Garuda and Rajinda laughed again, "Well, you don't expect us to look thousands of years old do you?" asked Rajinda. "When you die you slowly return to the prime of life, so if you die a very old person you will slowly progress backward, or if you die as a child or baby you will progress at your natural rate until you look our age or so, and then remain that way eternally."

Ileana asked cautiously, "We don't have any children, but two years ago I had a still-born baby girl. Would, would she be in heaven?"

Raj cautioned, "Ileana, don't…"

But Rajinda was smiling, "Yes, she is here. Would you like to meet her?"

"Yes, I, I would, please," Ileana said with tears in her eyes.

An Indian woman suddenly appeared holding the hand of a two-year-old girl, who looked just like her mother. The little girl looked into the camera and cried out, "Mommy!" Both Raj and Ileana recognized her in their hearts as their daughter and were crying now. "We know you didn't name her, and actually you weren't even allowed to see her when she was born, as the doctors took her away quickly. This lady looking after your daughter is named Ushmil, and Ushmil had been a still-born baby born about 170 years ago and she loves children."

Ushmil said, "I named your daughter, Aashirya, which means 'from the land of God.' I hope you are fine with that. I felt so honored to be raising your daughter and I show her pictures of both of you all the time."

Both Raj and Ileana said, "Aashirya." "Thank you, that is a beautiful name. Thank you for loving her." Raj continued with his eyes tearing up.

Raj bent over and clicked screen capture so they would have a picture of their girl.

Raj said, "Garuda and Rajinda, I'm sorry for doubting you, but these days you have to be very careful. And this is pretty fantastic! I guess I believe in what you are saying now. What would you like us to do?"

Garuda began, "In the Tammy show in America, that was the beginning, and now we would like to continue the education. America is mostly a Christian nation, so people might assume that you have to be Christian to go to heaven. But it doesn't work that way. It is not what religion you believe in that matters most or even what your concept of God is, but how you live your life. How much you love others or how much you purposely hurt others affects where you go in the spirit world. God is the source of all love and life and the more your character resembles God's nature, the higher you will be in the spirit world. Also God does not condemn evil people to hell, or for that matter, send them to heaven. In the spirit world like attracts like, so you will go to a realm that you resemble the most, based on what your heart is like. You judge yourself; God does not judge you. I explained earlier that I went to the blackest of hell when I died and yet now I am in this place of love and beauty. Nobody is condemned to eternal hell, but based on your efforts to help others rise to new levels, or to help people on Earth resist a temptation or make a better decision, your spirit grows to the point where you can finally advance to the next higher level."

Raj said, "Wow!" and paused, "OK, how can we help you?"

"There are a couple of things we would like your assistance with, first, Ileana's father has an important position with a television station and can decide what programs run. We would like you two to be the spirit hosts on a television show, similar to what happened in America. And second, you are what is known as a web master, is that right? That is what you do at your work, right?" questioned Garuda.

"Yes, I design and maintain the corporate web page." Raj explained.

"We would like you to set up a web site where anyone can ask questions and we can provide the answers, again where possible. We can send you pictures and videos taken in the spirit world and you can post those on the site. What you don't realize yet, is you live in the most incredible time. This is something God and the higher levels of the spirit world have been working towards for a long, long time. Now with the internet and television, international phones, and all this amazing technology the whole world can be educated together. Instead of people going to hell for thousands of years, now people can learn and grow very quickly on Earth and do it all together. How we live on Earth has a direct relationship with how we will begin our life in the spirit world," Rajinda said.

Ileana who had been transfixed watching her daughter play on the grass behind the couple looked up and asked, "You talk of God, but in our Hindu belief there are thousands or even millions of gods. How do explain that?"

Rajinda continued, "In the Tammy show, even though it was produced in basically a Christian nation, the spirit hosts, Daniel and Martha, did not talk about Jesus. They are good friends of ours, by the way, and we are working together. But it made some people upset, as you saw. All religions have some of the truth, but no religion has had the whole truth. There is only one God, and yet in Hinduism there is some amazing truth reveal in your scriptures.

God has worked through the religions to elevate mankind's consciousness and to encourage people to seek God and to live lives of goodness. The founders of the different religions had very deep experiences with God or with the divine but then after many years the religions tend to stray away from what the founders taught and gain a life of their own, creating dogma, ceremonies, traditions and creeds that often have little resemblance to the original message. We will not be promoting any religion, but only sharing what is true. We will share more deeply on this point in the show."

Ileana said, "You told me yesterday that my Dad would be having an interesting dream. Did that happen?"

Garuda laughed, "Yes, it was rather cryptic, but once you approach him with the idea for a show, like the Tammy Show, he will begin to understand what the dream was about. Or he will have another dream to help push him, if needed. Remind him that the Tammy Show had a record breaking audience as the word quickly got out, and that will help."

The "Talk with Aamir Show"

An interview-based TV show produced in Bangalore, India, "Talk with Aamir Show" has had celebrities, politicians, sports stars, business leaders and even gurus and yogis on the guest list. Aamir Jani was serious but with a good sense of humor, and generally viewed with great credibility.

Raj and Ileana Kumar had made the request for a show to Ileana's father a few days later and to their surprise he had readily agreed as long as they could guarantee that the hosts would actually show up from the Spirit World. He did not tell them of the three dreams he had experienced for the last three nights nor did Raj and Ileana mention that they knew he was going to be encouraged in this way. Ileana's father, Maneesh wanted to promote the show for a couple of weeks first to build up the anticipation and it was agreed that Raj and Ileana could be the Earth side guests, so they first got permission from Hewlett-Packard so as to not jeopardize their jobs.

Raj worked with Garuda and Rajinda along with Joseph Fourier, the French scientist, and some other spirit side engineers through his computer in the evenings after work to design the webpage and have it ready to launch right after the show. They were also told to connect with New Shambles, Inc. in the United States to work together on content and also so everything could be covered and approved by the legal department of New Shambles. Both "The Tammy Show" and the "Talk with Aamir Show" spirit world shows would be uploaded in their entirety, along with the video that first went viral with Jerry and Shambles, the dog. There would be a chat room and a place for people to ask questions. All questions would be addressed but not all could be answered, such as Raj's earlier request to "Show me God." And most astounding, some questions would be answered with live video feed from someone in the Spirit World.

As far as working with the general population, requests to find someone who had died and was now in the Spirit World, that would have to be dealt with in a sensitive way. For now they put up a statement on the site that they would not be retrieving any particular person from the spirit world. At this time the only response possible would be to ask the person on Earth looking for someone in spirit world to pray for that individual, for their growth and advancement to higher realms.

We knew some people would refuse to believe that their relatives, friends, ancestors, or even famous people they were inquiring about did not all go to the brighter areas after death. We also knew that not all in the spirit world would want to show up on a casual request, such as: if thousands of women all over the world wanted to personally talk with Elvis or one of the Beatles. That would be up to Elvis or any other celebrity whether they wanted to respond.

One very necessary reason for opening up inter-realm communication was for the working out of problems, for confessions of hurting someone and of being hurt, for forgiveness, for growth both on Earth and for those in the spirit realms. Most people in the Spirit World did not clear up all the problems they had on Earth before their passing. When we were ready for inter-realm meetings, we would encourage spirits who love counseling and mediating between parties to assist in any interchange between wronged individuals. There are millions of good souls who love to help people and this is a wonderful opportunity for them to assist people to resolve these blocks to their growth. The counselors would also benefit and would eventually be able to grow to a new level.

It had been three months since the Tammy Show and many people in the world were wondering about the promised "shows all over the world with different speakers from the spirit side who speak the local language and who come from the local customs and religions." So when Maneesh began promoting the coming spirit world communication TV show for Saturday, October 16, 2021 it was one of the easiest promotions he had ever done. Millions all over the world were waiting for the next event. But Maneesh was thorough and even arranged with Tammy McNeal to promote his coming show, which she did enthusiastically. Several stations in the United States, plus about 50 stations in various countries scheduled to run the show live or rebroadcast it at a more appropriate time so it would not be in the middle of the night, depending on the location. It was not that suddenly all of these television station owners around the world were having God experiences, but rather they could smell a winning program that would draw huge audiences.

October 16 was a muggy day in Bangalore, but towards evening it was cooler. Raj and Ileana were at the studio by 6 p.m. for the 8 p.m. show and met with Maneesh and Aamir Jani along with some of the upper management. The management was concerned about radical Hindu and Muslim elements of society that had threatened the show and arranged police protection for the station for the evening. The police swept the building and all cars in the parking lot with dogs sniffing for bombs. The guests for the show were to arrive an hour early and were prescreened for any criminal or fanatical histories and all were patted down and had to walk through a metal detector.

The format was a little different than The Tammy Show, as Aamir Jani was at a desk when the cameras started rolling. The words, Talk with Aamir Show, were written in script on the screen with sitar music in the background. When the introduction was finished Aamir introduced himself and the day's show: "Hello everyone, I am Aamir Jani, and today we have the long awaited continuation of what started with The Tammy Show in America a few months ago." The audience responded with great enthusiasm and applause. He continued, "In our studio today we have Raj and Ileana Kumar, who I understand were approached by a couple in the land after death with the promise that they will join us and tell us more of what we all have to look forward to when we leave this world. This show is being broadcasted live in many countries throughout the world. Welcome Raj and Ileana. Can you tell us your story and what we can expect on the show today?"

Ileana began, "My husband and I both work at the Hewlett-Packard corporate office in Bangalore and my father works for this station, C-Bangalore Channel 4 Television, as a producer. I guess, because of these connections and of our technical knowledge this group from what they call the spirit world approached us. We have met with the couple through our computers several times, and especially my husband has been working closely with them on something very exciting that we will tell you about later in the show."

Raj added, "Our lives have been transformed by this experience and we hope that many people throughout the world will also be able to connect to what is being offered to us. This show is not about us, though, and we would like to introduce our friends, Garuda and Rajinda. Are you there?"

On the large screen behind them Garuda and Rajinda came into view. They were sitting on large embroidered pillows on a mountain plateau with a beautiful view of a valley leading down to a large body of water. They both wore shimmering white robes that seemed to sparkle with color that was constantly moving in dazzling patterns. There was a gasp from the audience and many began to clap.

"Welcome to The Talk with Aamir Show, Garuda and Rajinda. It is an honor to finally meet you. Please tell us something about yourselves." Aamir said.

Both Garuda and Rajinda bowed from their waists with their hands pressed together, and Garuda said, "Namaste. The honor is ours to meet you and to be able to address people all over the world. Thank you, Aamir, for having us on your show. Our good friends Daniel and Martha Everheart gave you the initial introduction to the spirit realms and we would like to continue the sharing. My wife, Rajinda, and I did not know each other while we lived on the Earth over 5,000 years ago. My name used to be Jéagugun, meaning the Terrible One, and I was a tribal leader in Karnataka Rain Forest in southern India. Of course, India was not a nation then. We were cannibals who would feast on the blood and flesh of enemy tribes and I was especially vicious, without compassion for anyone else. I went to the blackest of hell full of warriors just like me and for over a thousand years we would fight each other in the most horrible ways, ripping and tearing at each other. That hell still exists today."

Rajinda added, "I was a devote Hindu, and so I went to a much better place in the Spirit World. To grow to higher levels you must help others, and so a group of us went down to the deepest hell. In one of our excursions there I felt a man questioning why he was there and wondering if there was anything more than this horrific existence. It took a few hundred years for Jéagugun to make progress to a higher place and finally he was growing quicker than I was. During this long process we began to love each other and finally were married by a Hindu priest in a realm of light. Before we married Jéagugun changed his name from The Terrible One to Garuda, meaning celestial white-crested eagle."

A shoe came flying toward the screen and a man from the audience stood up and shouted, "Allah condemns you for this blasphemy!" He was quickly subdued by security who were standing all around the audience and he was taken from the studio. As he was escorted out he shouted again, "A fatwa will be declared, all of you must die."

Aamir said, "Well we tried to make sure this didn't happen, but it is hard to know everything about everyone we let in. I know there have been protesters outside the station and threats online. But we felt this was too important to be intimidated. And with that segue maybe it is appropriate to ask, in "The Tammy Show" they showed a little of heaven, I wonder if it would also be good to see some of this hell you speak of, to give us perspective. What do you think?"

Garuda and Rajinda looked at each other and nodded in agreement. "We will not show you the deep hell like where I lived for over a thousand years," said Garuda, "but we will show you a gray level. We don't want to scare anyone and I am sure there are many children watching all over the world, but this will be scary enough. We will show you a place where no one presently living on Earth will recognize anyone they see as these people died hundreds of years ago."

Suddenly all the color was gone and in the dark there were hideous men and women in vile rags fighting over rocks and dirt. There were no plants, no greenery, nothing beautiful anywhere. Although no one could smell the scene you felt like it had the stench of rotten decay. One man with cruel bulging eyes and a patch of filthy hair clawed at the dirt and screeched, "this is my gold, get away from it, you pigs!" Immediately the others piled on him tearing his clothes, one woman who had only one tooth grabbed one of the rocks and ran away cackling, "it's mine, I'm rich!" Some of the crowd chased after the woman and others kept attacking the man, beating him, biting him.

The scene returned to the beautiful mountainside, the vibrant colors of the sky with birds flying around and the shining water below and of Garuda and Rajinda looking very serious. The audience let out a deep sigh of relief. Ileana said, "When Garuda and Rajinda first approached Raj and me they showed us a similar scene, not fighting over dirt, but of people who used to be bankers and others who only cared for money. They were in a very similar level."

Rajinda said, "Whatever we love that becomes our god, our passions define us. We want people to understand that they need to make sure their priorities are right. Those people loved only gold and in their lives and had murdered others to steal their gold. Now they see rocks and dirt as gold and anyone near them as people trying to take their gold from them. They do not care for anyone else, nor do they have any understanding of God or of love and compassion."

Raj asked, "Rajinda and Garuda, you said you would answer a question we had about Hindus believing in many gods on this show. Can you address that now?"

Rajinda replied, "I told you when I met Garuda I was a devote Hindu so let me explain about religions. All of the good religions on Earth today have been guided by God to give them the desire to seek for God and encourage people to live lives of goodness. But it is the nature of religion to believe only your religion is the truth, and that all others are false.

The religions are like spokes on a wheel as different paths to the center, to God. All religions have some of the truth, but none had all the truth. The religions were necessary to elevate mankind and this world from godlessness and darkness to seek for light. But at some point your blind belief in your religion can become a block to your spiritual growth."

"We know that what we are saying here will cause a lot of trouble in the world, but it must be said, for now is the time to remove the blocks and to find simple truth. There is only one true God. God is the source of all life and all that is good. God is the source of love. God is our parent, our father and our mother and as our parent you can ask God to share His divine love with you and to help you become a loving person. If your belief in your religion helps you to find God, then it is good and you should continue in your belief. But know that someone of another religion is also a sincere person looking for God, looking for truth, looking for love. And for those people who do not believe in anything spiritual, know that they are also a son and daughter of God, and so deserve love and respect. Also, love all creatures and love this Earth as the beautiful home we were given to cherish."

"In the realm that Garuda and I now live in all the people there have gone beyond their Earthly beliefs and now have a very simple philosophy, love and be thankful to God for all things and treat all living things, and especially all people with love and respect."

Garuda added, "In some of the realms of light in the Spirit World there are still the same Earthly religions, and even the same denominations meeting in their houses of worship. There are Sunni and Shiite Mosques; there are Catholic and all the different Protestant Churches; there are Jewish Synagogues; there are Buddhist and Hindu Temples, and on and on. We would like to show you one area that actually has twelve houses of worship of different religions."

Garuda and Rajinda then appeared in a vast plaza with twelve immense and transcendent houses of worship representing twelve major religions surrounding the central area. There was a Catholic cathedral, Muslim mosque, Jewish synagogue, Buddhist temple, Hindu temple, Orthodox Christian church, Zoroastrian fire temple, Sikh Gurdwara, evangelical Christian church, Taoist temple, Confucian temple, and Baha'i temple. People would appear in the plaza and enter their house of worship or disappear after existing them. Many of the parishioners wore clothes befitting their religion while others had on robes, similar to the one Garuda and Rajinda wore, white but with living colors moving around the cloth. People from the different religions would approach and greet other parishioners of other religions, some would hug each other, and all were respectful and smiling.

A Catholic priest and a Muslim imam, on seeing Garuda and Rajinda, paused their conversation and came over to greet them. "Oh, what an honor to greet such a beautiful couple, Garuda and Rejinda. What brings you here? And what kind of instrument are these men carrying?" asked the Imam.

"Shaykh Ibrahem, so good to see you again," said Garuda, "We have a live audience on the Earth watching us as we show your magnificent houses of worship. This is a camera our scientist invented that is able to project to computers on Earth and from there to televisions all over the world."

Imam Ibrahem said, "I have no idea what you are talking about, I have not kept up with the inventions on the Earth side. You say people are watching us from there?"

Laughing Rajinda replied, "That's right, do you have anything to say to the world?"

"Well, yes I do, love God with all your heart and love all people, no matter what their faith is." Imam Ibrahem responded.

"That sounds a lot like what Jesus says," Rajinda observed.

"Yes, we all love Jesus here, along with Mohammed and the Buddha, and all the great saints who have helped us find God or Allah," said the Imam.

"Amen to that," Father McCoy joined in. They all laughed together. With that Garuda and Rajinda said farewell to their friends and were then immediately right back on their mountain.

Garuda continued, "As you can see all the religions are aware and respect each other, and people still find comfort in believing in their religion, in their community of faith and that is good. We showed you this to inspire all the religions of the world to have the same kind of mind, the same love and respect for all seekers of all faiths. There is no conversion from one religion to another here in the Spirit World, no competition for souls to save."

Aamir, who was spiritual and yet, more secular and intellectual, interjected, "Well, this is extremely informative. Does anyone in the audience have questions for our honored guests?"

A middle-aged lady in a nice red sari stood up and a microphone was brought to her. She asked, "If this God you speak of is so good, why does he send people to hell? In Hinduism we know there are some gods that bring prosperity when we honor them, some that bring a good harvest and some that bring destruction and chaos and this explains why the world has both the good and bad. We also know there are good spirits and evil spirits all around us."

Rajinda answered, "Like we said before, all religions have some truth, in Hinduism you will find some incredible wisdom in the Bhagavad Gita, Upanishads, Vedas and Sutras that have helped to guide people for thousands of years. Here is a nice quote from the Srimad Bhagavatam, 'Like the bee, gathering honey from different flowers, the wise man accepts the essence of different scriptures and sees only the good in all religions.' So you see, we are not disparaging Hinduism or any religion, all are from God. But God did not create hell, nor does God condemn people to hell. God created us to be co-creators with Him and unless we ask, God will not interfere with what we have created. We created this hell on Earth where people of different faiths kill each other in God's name just as those you saw in hell earlier created their own hell. These have nothing to do with God for God is only good, only pure love."

Aamir said, "Garuda and Rajinda it has been such an honor to share my show with you. Do you have any final words for the audience?"

"You live in the most amazing time in human history. You no longer have to go blindly fearing your death and then struggling for a long time to grow in the land of spirits. God is your first parent, your greatest father and your greatest mother and has been working towards this time to bring an end to ignorance, to let you know that He/She loves you more than you have ever known and wants to embrace every person." Rajinda responded.

Aamir continued to draw the show to a close, "Raj and Ileana, you said you had something you wanted to share at the end of the show. That time has arrived. What have you got?"

Raj responded, "At Hewlett-Packard I set up and maintain the corporate website. That is one of the reasons Ileana and I were chosen. I have been working with Garuda and Rajinda and others in the spirit realms to set up a website, which will answer questions about the spirit world. Today's show along with The Tammy Show will be on the site and also that first video that went viral about Shambles the dog and Jerry, some of you may have seen. I've been working with New Shambles in America on the content. There will be a Q&A section, where answers will be supplied from knowledgeable people in the spirit world to me that I will then put on the site. Other videos and pictures from the spirit world will be sent to me to also add and I will set up pages for the different topics."

"Wow, that is incredible!" proclaimed Aamir.

Raj continued, "The one issue we are not ready to launch is when people ask about specific people: relatives, ancestors, friends, celebrities or famous people and where they are in the spirit realms or if they want to connect with them. That will take far more man-power to deal with than I can manage with requests coming from all over the world. But if Google or Facebook wants to lend their man and computing power and server space I would be happy to partner with them. But also we have been informed that this issue is very sensitive, as some people who were thought to be wonderful people were actually not and did not go to the level in Spirit World where people thought they would. Many people might get quite hostile when they hear the truth. But the initial website will be quite amazing and at some time we will deal with connecting people with their departed loved ones. This initial site is called, RebirthInSpirit.org and will be live as soon as this show is over." As Raj was speaking the words: www.RebirthInSpirit.org was scrolling across the bottom of the screen.

Aamir laughed, "Well I hope you have a powerful server because it is going to swamped by people logging in from all over the world at the same time."

Raj grinned and grimaced at the same time, "Well, we have partnered with New Shambles, Inc. and have set up many volunteers in America and a few other countries. But yes, I know it may well crash at first, but eventually it will calm down and hopefully become manageable."

Aamir ended the show with, "Thank you to all our friends in the spirit world, to Garuda and Rajinda, to our guests here, Raj and Ileana, to our wonderful audience here in the studio and to all viewers all over the world. This has been the Talk with Aamir Show. Good night and bless you all."

Chapter 8
Our Son, Samuel

Reaching Out to Samuel

Martha and I met with Jerry, Jill's son, who was the first person revealed on a computer monitor from the spirit world. We shared about the life of our son and the consequences of that terrible life by his present life in hell. Jerry was particularly fond of us as we worked hard to help him advance from hell to the beautiful place he now lives in. He has helped Jiva Satata tremendously and we were deeply grateful to him as well.

Right after the Amir show we took this time for an important mission. Martha sensed that a change had come about with our son, a feeling of regret for the first time for the life he lived. We thought of Samuel and desired to see him. We prepared our minds for the onslaught and the three of us were immediately brought into a suffocating darkness. A lake of tar with flames dancing over the surface was surrounded by black burnt hills. We saw figures in the tar writhing and reaching out, wailing that sent shivers down my spine. There were skeletal trees in the hills, many with figures hanging from them, living tormented souls who could not be killed again. We heard shouts and screams and a gang of vicious men ran past us. "Samuel!" Martha yelled out and I realized one of the gang was our son.

At first the young man turned and glared at us, hissing, expecting a challenge. "Samuel, I am your mother," Martha said more calmly, but with tears in her eyes. Samuel, finally recognizing us, hid his face and turned from us hiding his hideous form.

"What do you want? Go away. I don't want to see you. Why are you here? Don't look at me! Don't look at me!" Samuel cried out. "Who is with you?"

"Samuel, I am your father and Jerry is our friend," I said.

Samuel glanced maliciously at me quickly and said, "The bastard father who wasn't there when mother had such a hard life. I don't want to see you ever. Did you bring a slave with you to carry me off?"

I stepped back and let Martha approach him. "We are here to help you, Sam," she said.

At that moment three revolting thugs came running at us, and Samuel instinctively jumped in front of Martha protecting her. Jerry also jumped in and blocked the attackers. I walked over and allowing our light to shine forth in the darkness and with force said, "Be gone! We are from heaven and you cannot touch us." Cowering and hiding their eyes they slinked away.

Samuel glanced at Jerry with a little more respect asked, "Who are you?"

"I am friends of your parents and I owe my life to them. My name is Jerry. Recently your parents came and found me in hell and began reaching out to me," Jerry responded.

"You helped this man before you helped me?" Samuel spat out looking at me with such hatred.

"Sam, I am very sorry I wasn't there for you and your mother. I tried to help you from the spirit side but you always resisted. For so many years I couldn't approach you in the spirit world and had to wait for your mother," I said. "You have too much resentment and anger towards me. We also came at this time because we felt a softening in your heart. There has to be some opening on your part before we can help you."

"Like I need your help. I'll talk with Mother and this man can stay, but I'm not ready for you," Samuel shot back.

I retreated and let them talk while I sent loving thoughts to surround them. After a long while Martha and Jerry returned and I could feel from Martha they had made some progress.

We visualized our home and soon were back in our loving home. We all breathed a sigh of relief and let the goodness of this land fill us with its healing essence. The sun was shining through the window carrying the smell of the many blossoms in our garden. Our work to help Samuel had finally begun.

Chapter 9
Our Work on Earth

New Shambles, Inc.

In the months since The Tammy Show by our encouragement from spirit world, New Shambles was ready to take off, along with assisting with the efforts in India; they were ready to have more shows. From that original Thanksgiving meeting, Edwin, Jackie Nagorski, Mike Templeton, Ben Stine and Jill Tanner had to quit their jobs and devout all of their attention to the tsunami of requests from all over the world to appear on other guest shows, as now paid guests, along with their spirit friends. We in the spirit realms, of course, did not have any need for money, transportation or lodging, which was a great bonus to any show we were on.

Using the people who were at the Thanksgiving meeting Edwin, now the CEO hired Mike Templeton, with his good looks and easy manner, to join Jackie Nagorski as a presenter on future shows. Edwin knew he was not a good host opted out of going on any other shows. Ben Stine was hired as New Shambles' business manager, Jill Tanner, Jerry's mom, was the Filming Manager and videographer, and Patrick, Ben's son, who was now 19 and had at least graduated from high school, became the system IT Manager.

This was all through our encouragement from the spirit side to go professional so they could devote their energy to this undertaking and be able to make a living through the work. This quickly became a very lucrative business. They leased a large office in Oakland that included a TV studio and purchased desks, office equipment along with broadcasting cameras and equipment to produce their own shows. They hired a professional promoter who began reaching out to the big players, HBO, ABC, Netflix and others. Their legal department also grew to handle international conflicts.

In January, 2022 to the shock of the New Shambles crew, Edwin's longtime friends, Stan and Irene Peterson, who had left the Thanksgiving party in disgust showed up at their office. This was not a surprise to Martha and me, as we had been focusing our love on Stan since he left. Stan began, looking a lot more humble than he had in 2020, "Look, I'm very sorry we doubted your work. You know me, I am a scientist, and have to see proof before I can believe in anything new."

Edwin raised his eyebrows and asked, "OK, we are very happy to see you both, and did you get that proof?"

"Well most people our age know someone who has died, our parents, certainly our grandparents, some friends, some coworkers. For the past few months I was having a repeating dream, my mom is still alive, but my dad died a few years back of emphysema, being a lifelong smoker. I kept seeing my dad begging me to pray for him. But I didn't even believe in God, let alone life after death, so I just felt these dreams were from an emotional feeling since your Thanksgiving gathering," Stan began. "Then Irene starting having the same dream, my dad asking her to pray for him and to help me believe it was real. My dad always loved Irene like his own daughter since we started going together."

Irene added, with tears in her eyes, "Stan's dad, Phil, told me in these dreams some things that Stan had done that I never knew, never suspected. So I asked Stan about them and told him where I got the information, and that shocked us both. It has taken us so long to come to you because we had some personal issues to work out first. And well, we now believe in life after death. We came to apologize and hopefully be friends again."

Edwin reached out and hugged them both together and Mike who had seen them come in joined in the group hug. "Please don't tell me the details on your marital issues. Of course we are friends, we always were."

Irene smiled weakly and said, "Thanks, Edwin, we appreciate that."

Edwin continued, "In fact, we could sure use your help here if you are looking for a job."

Stan replied, "I have four more months to work at Micro Sun International to be able to retire at the minimum age to get a reasonable pension, but then, if the offer is still open I would love to help in your work. Irene is in between jobs and she is available and she is an excellent Human Resources Manager."

Edwin said, "For our growing company we are in need of a HR Director. When can you start? And Stan you are the best videographer I know, that position will be open for you when you are ready. You would work with Jill. In fact if you and Jill can begin working on a better promo that we could to show the studios, you can start right away as a freelancer."

The World Begins to Wake Up

There was a great divide in response to the Talk with Aamir Show and to the website, RebirthInSpirit.org. Those who were more moderate in their belief system were more ready to accept this new message, but many who were more conservative in their religious devotion or those who had more to lose, dug their heels in and became even more fanatical and narrow.

Once again there were demonstrations against what had been revealed on the show in almost every nation, but this time there were some counter demonstrations that had accepted what we were sharing. This division was necessary in the steps towards reconciling the two sides in the future. It was better to be hot or cold on this most important revelation rather than non-committal for it is their eternal life that was in the balance.

RebirthInSpirit.org had record-breaking hits from the moment it became live and continued to have astronomical number of visitors. Raj called New Shambles in America and asked if they could connect with Jerry and ask him if he could take charge of the website from the spirit side, since he was more familiar with the computers and the internet than any of us who had been here for hundreds or thousands of years. Jerry became the technical advisor for the site and Martha and I helped decide the content, what things to make videos or photographs of and how to answer many of the questions. We created a new team who would be focused on creating the videos in the spirit realms, of conducting interviews, filming events, and of everyday life and we gave them the assignments and then reviewed what they brought to us.

Martha asked me one day, "Dan, can you help me answer these questions from the site on reincarnation and past-life regressions?" And we knew the questions would be never ending. There were so many contradictory beliefs in the world all adding to the confusion. It was time to wake up, shake things up, and begin the healing.

Huge numbers of people wanted Jesus, Moses or Buddha to show up on the website or on one of the television shows. But we were told, and already knew, that would cause more problems and would not help the cause, not at this stage. The Islamic world was far less embracing of this whole concept and there were not many requests for Mohammed to

show himself and in fact, there was a rise in terrorist attacks and condemnation from Muslims against the "infidels" and this new "Satanic"
deception invading the world. Tammy McNeal, Aamir Jani and New
Shambles all had to hire security. But as more shows were produced and
the message became more widespread that dissipated the focus and the
threat away from the original shows.

Chapter 10
Jiva Satata

Meeting with Jiva Satata

Garuda and Rajinda sent out a thought for all involved in this stage of the work of Jiva Satata to have a meeting. Anselma Glaus, the celebration organizer, was asked to make it a festive occasion, but also everyone knew it involved some serious planning on implementation of the next phase. Anselma selected The Grande Riunioni Hall as the venue for the meeting as it had a large enough meeting room and a beautiful view overlooking a shimmering lake fed by three waterfalls. No one in the spirit realms has to eat to live, but for those masters chefs who love to cook it was always a great pleasure to prepare dishes that bring joy to all who partake. The Grande Riunioni was renowned for its Italian cooks and for the variety of exquisite pastas and wines. Anselma also planned an historical reenactment as entertainment for our break.

Some of the topics to discuss were:

• Discuss the shows and what was taught on them, what is the reaction

• How to influence the greatest number of people by reaching important leaders

• What the website was offering, what videos were playing, what questions were being asked?

• When to start the phase of opening up the spirit world to any personal computing device and how should that take place?

• How to reach out to people in countries that limit television and internet access?

By the Earthly calendar the meeting was set for February 6th and 7th, 2022 and people who were responsible for different aspects of the outreach were asked to prepare a report. Forty people representing the core staff were invited including someone representing each of the main religions on Earth. Martha and I were asked to speak on the shows that New Shambles has participated in so far. Joseph Fourier wanted to ask whether to multiply the instruments for making videos or to create a hall for spirits to come to speak to the recipients on Earth in order to keep it centralized with the same message and under control. Jerry would report on the website. There would be discussion on influencing people with dreams and even visions.

Once these reports were given, the main topic would be on how to speed up acceptance that this was authentically from the Spirit World and more importantly was God's desire. We would also look at who were the most influential people on Earth to reach out to. On the religious side there were a few obvious choices of people to focus on, the Pope, the Dalai Lama, top evangelical leaders, but there was no one person leader for the Muslims or for the Jews, Hindus, Sikhs, Buddhists or Protestant Christianity. Other people from other non-religious disciplines would also be considered, such as: influential people in political positions, academics, entertainment or sports.

Most of the participants for the meeting began showing up on the lawn outside The Grande Riunioni Hall a half hour to an hour before the meeting was to begin, just to have time to see friends and to share together. One more recent couple to the spirit world, Fred and Sally Anderson, representing evangelical Christianity came motoring up over the grass in a beautiful red automobile, which we were told was a replica of a 1939 Jaguar SS100, which meant nothing to the majority there. Since everyone in spirit world travels by thought there are no roads like on Earth, but if you love cars you can certainly have them, and Mr. Anderson has an excellent collection. It doesn't run on gasoline, but rather on thought power, and doesn't create any pollution, nor does anything else in our realms.

Once everyone was assembled a blessing was said and dinner was served first. In the spirit realms no animals are used for meat, but rather substances that have the taste and texture of shrimp, chicken, pork or beef had been created for our culinary delight.

Garuda and Rajinda come from a higher realm than most assembled, but there was never a feeling that they were better than anyone else. They loved our company and we loved theirs. Once the refreshments were over they stood and holding hands sang a song that spoke of traversing great mountains and overcoming many obstacles all for love. As they sang, a beautiful dome of marvelous interacting colors surrounded them. Music and color are always intertwined here, especially harmonic music. At the conclusion their performance of love was awarded with a standing ovation.

Now that the atmosphere was elevated Garuda began the meeting. "Friends, we are gathered here because of the great undertaking that

God has asked us to do. Some of you know that the science and technology for establishing communication for those living on the Earth has advanced for the last one hundred and fifty years. It has been more than two years since the Earth was made aware of our efforts to communicate. We called this meeting to assess our efforts so far and to prepare the next phase of our global outreach."

Rajinda added, "Our purpose is to show the world that there is one loving God and that our lives on Earth are very important. It is on Earth that we learn of love and that we begin to have the concept of family, first in our own families and then to the whole of mankind as one extended family. Every person on Earth needs love and healing, as there has been a lot of suffering for all of our long history."

Garuda said, "We would like to first hear some reports from different aspects of the campaign and then we will focus on how to proceed from here. Daniel and Martha Everheart, can you tell of the different shows that New Shambles has put on and what the response has been?

I began, "Everyone is aware of the first appearance on The Tammy Show in California in 2020, so I won't go over that one again. That was the only show where Martha and I were the spirit side hosts so far. After that initial show, New Shambles was on the very popular Today Show in New York and we asked the Jewish couple, Lev and Ruth Goldstein to host that one. Lev and Ruth lived in Russia in the 1500s. We wanted each show to have different spirit side hosts to give a different perspective of spirit life, and yet from the Earth side after the first show with Edwin and Jackie as hosts, it has since been Jackie Nagorski and Mike Templeton who were the hosts to give the audience some consistency."

"After the Today Show they went back to The Tammy Show. This time Tammy's studio was much too small so they had it outside at the Hollywood Bowl with over 26,000 in attendance. We asked the priest, Father Sean McCoy, who happened to be on your Indian show representing the Catholic faith when you went to the Plaza of the Religions, to host that show along with Anselma Glaus, so there would also be someone from Jiva Satata there."

Martha added, "That was quite a show, both Father McCoy and Anselma are very good entertainers and Anselma gave an amazing testimony as an early Christian and that contrasted with Father McCoy who was in Ireland in the 1900s under the powerful Catholic Church." At the table, Father McCoy and Anselma smiled and gave a wave of acknowledgement. Martha continued, "We always have both a man and a woman as our hosts so it is balanced in our presentation and also in the reception from the audience."

I continued, "After the second Tammy Show, New Shambles went international. They hosted a show in Hungary, Thailand and Brazil so far. In Thailand we used our Buddhist friend, Qieci[4], a Chán monk who lived in China from 904 to 989 CE. He was paired with a Shinto priestess, Ueno Nagora, who assisted a Shogun in the 14th century Japan. The response has been mixed, in general positive, but in each location there has also been protests, some violent."

"In Thailand a Buddhist monk committed self-immolation, setting himself on fire as a protest against our message of inclusion of all religions. We might expect that from other religions but were surprised that a Buddhist would protest inclusiveness. He is in a recovery room in this level of spirit world, and it might be another month before he is ready to be awoken. As you know, after committing suicide in such a drastic way, it can take a while for the spirit to calm and he will need a lot of love and patience from some of the good people in the recovery room assisting him. He is very fortunate that his motivation for ending his life was for a higher good or he would not have ended up in this realm. We hope to teach him when he is ready and have him join us in a future broadcast. His face was broadcast all over the world on news stations, so it could be quite impactful if he was later brought on a show."

Rajinda said, "Yes, we are aware of him. Please let me know when he is awake. I would like very much to meet him and mentor him."

"Thank you, Rajinda, we certainly will." Martha responded.

Garuda said, "Thank you, Dan and Martha. Please keep working with New Shambles and put on more shows, especially internationally. We can see a very positive response growing throughout the world. We like Tammy McNeal. Have you considered bringing her with you to do a show outside the United States?"

I responded, "New Shambles is in talks with her to do just that. It would have to be worked out financially and it would certainly be a major boost to her show. Once they get past these Earthly issues, I think it will probably happen."

"Very good, thanks for all your work on this. Now we would like to hear from Jerry Tanner on the response to the website and also he has requested to help educate us on the value of computers and the internet and especially on using what is called social media," Garuda said.

We had been working with Jerry to improve his language and presentation, and he made us proud. Jerry stood up to applause and began, "I grew up in this modern age of computers and the internet. For those who lived before this time, I don't think you can grasp the power of this worldwide interconnectedness. Anyone anywhere in the world can be a friend with anyone else in the world whether you actually met them or not. The Internet has transformed the world and made the world much smaller in terms of communication more than any other invention. It has given anyone the power like the press held exclusively before, the power of information, the ability to help or hurt businesses, the ability to speak out when there is the abuse of power, the ability to post a video of police abusing a citizen or of a country abusing its people which can be viewed by anyone in the world, at least where the government hasn't restricted internet use."

Rajinda interjected, "That brings up a point we want to address in this conference, reaching out to people in China, North Korea and many Muslim countries where media access is limited. But sorry for the interruption, please continue."

Jerry continued, "What I would like to propose is that we go beyond what our one website, RebirthInSpirit.org can do. Sure, we have all the shows recorded on the site, but we can do much more if we open up an interactive site that allows people on Earth to have contact with anyone in the spirit world, like an inter-realm Facebook site. Facebook is where you designate who you want to be your friends and then they can see any post you put on your site, any statements, photos or video and you can see anything your friends post. Each person can directly communicate to say from 50 to a 1,000 friends through your cell phone or other computing device, which almost every one owns now. You can be at an event, video-recording it, and immediately that video with sound can be seen anywhere in the world. The whole world is very much interconnected. If we were to set up a site where anyone on Earth can connect to someone in the spirit world, that would greatly expand interconnectedness."

Garuda responded, "Since you bring up this issue, let me address it now and then I will let you finish later, Jerry, for there are some important concerns we have about opening up communication on such a level and this will affect our whole conversation. One of the problems throughout the ages before our present efforts to interact with the Earth have been that mediums or spiritually open people could not always discern whether a spirit they were speaking with was really the person they thought it was, or whether the spirit was from a higher level or from a lower level deceiving the person receiving the communication and leading them in the wrong direction."

"There are many very powerful evil spirits who presently interact with people on the Earth, or they control hundreds or thousands of other evil spirits to influence the Earth to go the path that will lead to the destruction of their souls. These evil forces are very aware of the effort we are doing, because although they can never come into the higher realms of the spirit world and affect our world, they can interact freely with anyone they can establish a common base with on the Earth, no matter if that person is overall a good person or not. Through people on Earth they have seen our shows, seen our website and know what is happening. They feel threatened that they will lose control over affecting people's destinies. Our work has not only stirred up the Earth but has also stirred up powerful evil forces on the spirit side.

That is one of the reasons you have seen the protests and the violence to our message, because of the influence from these evil spirits. The majority of people in all levels of the spirit world have no concern at all with the people on Earth or what is happening there, and there are others who are keenly aware and actively involved in what is happening on the Earth side."

"As we all know here, it is on Earth where there are billions of souls who have not clearly chosen a life of service and love for their fellow beings and if they don't change their lives will find they have ended up in a very dark spirit world. Our purpose is to make it very clear to everyone on Earth, that a life of loving God and loving people is the only true belief. If we open up communication freely to anyone in the spirit realms, it will not be long before there will be great deceivers pretending to be from higher realms or even more harmful, zealot religious followers in the spirit world who denounce our message of inclusiveness as evil and that only their views are from God."

"These are some of the issues that we deal with in the higher realms which include the founders of the major religions, who I might add, are greatly saddened to see their followers killing or enslaving others, including innocent children, in the name of their faith or in the name of God. We absolutely do not want to give any tools to those who have a contrary message. We therefore must control the spirit side technology and who has access to it. Evil spirits obviously cannot fool us, but they can fool millions who still have their physical lives."

"So far we have controlled the message from the spirit side and must continue to so. We want to keep the message of love, of a holy and absolutely involved God, of forgiveness, of hope that all people can and will eventually be in the highest heaven, that we are all brothers and sisters who deserve love and respect. I know that you all agree with these sentiments."

We all clamored to respond, "Here, here, absolutely, we agree, yes!" rang out. Many of us had not lived unselfish lives and had gone through the long grueling course of restoration through service in reaching out to those in darker hells to grow to where we were now, as had Garuda.

Garuda continued, "We like the idea of opening up communication and setting up a spirit to Earth interaction, but must limit it to this realm or higher, which greatly reduces who the people on Earth can speak to. It is possible that we can bring someone from a lower realm to this realm for the time it takes for a brief interaction and we will consider that when it serves a higher purpose. And on a related issue, what are everyone's thoughts on either setting up one location in the spirit realm for interaction or of duplicating the equipment so anyone in this realm can begin their own outreach?"

We are all equal in value as sons or daughters of God but our understanding of God's will and direction is not equal. The spirit realms are not democracies, since we are elevated not by our opinions but rather by our closeness to God and to reaching our own divinity, yet everyone appreciated that our thoughts on important issues were sought and respected.

Joseph Fourier stood up and addressed the assembled, "Over a hundred years ago I was put in charge of leading the efforts to develop the technology to communicate with the Earth and to find the right people to join in this work. I deeply appreciate the trust given to me and especially am grateful for the work of all the scientist and engineers both on the Earth side and on this side and of course many who passed from their physical lives joined us in our spirit side research later. It has been a wonderful chance to serve all mankind in this way. Our goal for the Earth was always that the technology and equipment would be available to most people alive and that day has come. But the spirit side was always a question. After listening to Garuda I would say that it would be better that we maintain control of the message and therefore keep control of the technology. At this point I would say it is too early to let it go freely. Everyone in this level and higher are good loving people, but we are also unique individuals and some are very strong willed with strong ideas." Everyone had a good laugh at that, each of us thinking of someone we knew.

Rajinda said, "Good and we agree. Joseph, can you arrange with the Master Architect to create a beautiful hall for reaching our brothers and sisters on the Earth. Put it near the Hall of Learning in that great field behind it. Now let's take a break and I know Anselma has some surprises for us. When we come back, Jerry, you can finish if you have more and then we will move on to reaching people who have repressive governments that don't allow free access to television shows and the Internet. While we are on break think of suggestions on what to call our new hall and then I would like to hear your ideas when we are back together."

Presentation of the Polos meeting Kublai Khan

Anslema Glaus stood up and announced, "During this break we have a special performance, a short reenactment from 1274 when Marco Polo journeyed from Venice with his father and uncle, Niccolo and Maffeo Polo and met with the Mongol leader, Kublai Khan, the grandson of Ghengis Khan in China. May I present, Marco, Niccolo, Maffeo Polo and Kublai Khan who will present a representation of that great meeting."

Marco, Niccolo, Maffeo Polo and Kublai Khan came in from a side room and gave a bow from the waist and Niccolo said, "Let me give you a little background for this play. My brother, Maffeo, and I had been to

China already and became very close to the Mongolian leader, Kublai Khan. After a few years we persuaded him that we needed to go back to our hometown of Venice, Italy. Kublai Khan had become interested in Christianity and asked us to bring a request to the Pope to send 100 priests who could teach grammar, rhetoric, logic, geometry, arithmetic, music and astronomy along with some holy oil from Jerusalem with us on our next visit. Well, his requests were more than we could accomplish and we could only find two priests, but those soon turned back as the journey became harder. But we did bring my son, Marco, who later wrote all about his adventures. I had never met my son until we returned to Venice where he was 15. When he was 17 years old we left for China and the trip took four years.[5] And now our little play."

Instantly the three Italian Polos had clothes that they had worn on that long journey over 700 years ago. They were on horses with a caravan of 15 servants along with four camels. We could see this happening as if it were their actual journey hundreds of years ago and this was actually a projection from their minds creating the scenery and the other players. As they were approaching Kublai Khan's summer palace in Shangdu, (near present-day Zhangjiakou), they stopped the caravan. Maffeo addressed the group, "We have been away from China for several years and we don't know what the political atmosphere is like or even if Kublai Khan is still alive and still in power. Let's change out of our traveling clothes and put on our formal clothes. You can be sure that runners have already gone to the palace to inform them that foreigners were coming. Don't mention Kublai Khan until we know if he is still in good stead here."

Some villagers walked by and Niccolo addressed them in Mandarin Chinese, both Niccolo and Maffeo spoke fluent Mongolian and Mandarin, having lived in Khan's court for over five years. Although they spoke in Chinese everyone in the audience could understand them, as in the spirit lands understanding comes to the mind of what a person is meaning to say, even if you can't understand the words. This once again shows the power of thought that is the overriding principle for all things in the spirit lands. "Good sirs," Niccolo began, "can you tell us who is the honorable leader of these lands?" Several of the villagers ran away, but one brave young man said, "Well, it is Kublai Khan, and you better not displease him or you will not leave this land with your head still on your shoulders."

The caravan was greatly relieved to hear that Kublai Khan was still in power or their long arduous trip could have ended suddenly very tragically with their deaths or enslavement.

Soon Mongol soldiers came riding fast on horses and surrounded the travelers. The soldiers surrounded the caravan riding in a large circle with swords and bows and arrows pointing at them. "Who are you and where do you come from, foreign devils?" a leader of the soldiers threatened. But before anyone could answer one of the soldiers shot one of the servants in the chest and he fell off his horse bleeding.

Suddenly there were horns blowing and they could see a procession approaching. There were several horses and marching soldiers kicking up dust and in the middle an ornately decorated elephant with a riding box on top. The procession stopped near the caravan and an elderly Mongolian man announced, "Bow before the mighty, Kublai Khan, ruler of the Middle Kingdom!" Everyone in the caravan prostrated himself on the ground, fearing to look up.

But then Niccolo and Maffeo heard a familiar voice, "Is that my good friends, the Italian brothers named Polo who left so many years ago?" Kublai was assisted out of the traveling box and down off the elephant and ran to his old friends. "My friends, you have returned. These are my honored guests, and they will be treated with the highest respect. I am sorry one of your servants was killed. Whoever did this will be punished and after he said this the soldier who shot the servant was knocked from his horse and was prostrating himself on the ground. My Italian friends, please rise and tell me of our travels."

Niccolo said, "Honored Khan, it is so good to see you again. Please spare the soldier's life, for he was only protecting your kingdom."

"Then for our friendship this man's life is spared, but he can no longer ride with my guard," said Khan.

Niccolo continued, "Emperor Khan, this is my son Marco. When I came to China all those years ago, I did not know my wife was pregnant. I met him for the first time when I returned to Venice. He is now 21 years old."

Marco bowed and said, "Respected leader, I am very glad to meet you. My father and uncle have told me so much of their long stay with you and of your generous heart and great leadership. I know you asked that we bring 100 priests to instruct your court of Christianity, but we were not able to do that. But I would be most honored to teach you many things having been well educated in Italy. We do have a letter from the leader of Christianity, the Pope, to you and have secured a jug of sacred oil from Jerusalem."

The scene faded away and everyone applauded enthusiastically. Kublai Khan then addressed the audience in the Grande Riunioni Hall, "With the first visit with the brothers, Niccolo and Maffeo Polo and then with their return with Marco, this had a great effect on China and Mongolia at that time. They stayed in my court for twenty years and I made Marco a governor of one province. This East/West meeting changed Europe and China as we learned so much from each other; technological, political and religious that helped both worlds. We are so glad that we could share this part of history with you today. Thank you."

Everyone stood up and cheered the participants, as we love the historical reenactments that are presented in the Spirit World, especially when the actual people who made history present them.

The Conference Continues

Rajinda stood up and addressed everyone, "Before we continue, did anyone think of a name for the grand building that will be built for our communication with the Earth?" Father McCoy called out "How about Nexus Magna, which is Latin for Great Connection?" "Oh, I like that," said Rajinda, "Did anyone else come up with a name?" I called out, "The Phoenix, because the phoenix dies and then is reborn. But I like Nexus Magna better," and after more discussion there was general agreement.

"Jerry, did you have more to report on the website?" asked Garuda.

Jerry stood up and said, "We have millions of people viewing RebirthInSpirit.org, so I know it is having a great impact. So far we have videos from our realm on how a house is built, on an orchestra performing with the color architecture forms swirling above the performance, of various animals unique to the spirit world, and lots of testimonies of people with a large variety of experiences, how they died and what it was like to awaken in the spirit world, of people going to lower realms and the lessons it took to make progress, of professional people translating their earthly experience to being able to do useful and appreciated work in the spirit realms. I would love to put in a video of the erecting of the new building, Nexus Magna. That would be wonderful. What other things would you like to see on the site?"

Martha stood up and suggested, "Could you give tours of the Hall of Art, Hall of Books and the Hall of Science? I think it would be amazing for people to see the great masterpieces, like Leonardo Da Vinci's 'The Last Supper' as it appeared in his mind and now in our Hall of Art for all eternity. Also, how about showing a class for children who died young now developing the skills to make roses and other flowers."

"Wow, good idea! We could do a whole section on children in the spirit world, how they got here and how they are educated. Absolutely and thanks." Jerry responded.

Rajinda stood up and said, "We appreciate all of your efforts and your teams out making the videos and how you have worked closely with the Earth side team and with New Shambles, and Raj from India, to make this amazing website. It has greatly helped our work of sharing the reality of our world with the people on the Earth side." Everyone applauded and cheered. Jerry had a big smile on his face and bowed his head.

Garuda stood and declared, "We have two more issues to address in this conference, one is reaching influential people and the next is starting a campaign into closed societies where news is controlled, such as; China, North Korea and many Muslim countries." Garuda chuckled, "These closed societies can censor and distort news coming in from outside their countries, and block any attempts to open them up, but they can't stop our efforts. Their borders, weapons and intimidations have no meaning to us. I'm sure we will become quite a frustration to them as their control is challenged."

Garuda continued, "Our next issue is identifying the most influential people and conducting a campaign to educate them about the importance of their life on Earth and the consequences of their actions later in their life in the Spirit World. For the Catholic Church it is not hard to make a plan with a single person, the Pope, who is revered by Catholics all over the world. What are the points that need to be clarified in Catholic belief that will help the one billion Catholics?"

Father Sean McCoy stood up and said, "There are a number of points that need adjusting, the image of God as judgmental, eternal fire and brimstone hell, the lifelong chastity of priests and nuns which leads to sexual frustration, the view of angels as more divine creations than people, the divinity of Jesus and his mother, Mary."

"Let's first focus on the image of God and that hell is the result of people's actions, not God's judgment. At this point we don't need to correct every misconception of every religion, but rather want to focus on helping people live their lives with love and compassion." Garuda added.

"Sean, can you set up a team to reach the Pope and all his advisors? You might consider enlisting former Popes, at least those who are in the higher realms along with other prominent Catholics, especially those who have been 'canonized as saints' by the church," Rajinda said.

"Wow! Here I was only a simple Irish priest and now I am responsible for the Pope, the Cardinals and the whole Roman Catholic Church! If my mother could only see me now, oh wait, she can since she came to the spirit world twenty years before I did," Sean McCoy said. Everyone laughed.

Rajinda continued, "Let us know how we can help at any stage in your work, especially when the Pope begins to come around and is willing to speak out to the world. Now let's move onto the Buddhist religion, the Dalai Lama is now in his late 80s and will not live much longer. But although there are many sects of Buddhism, he is well regarded by all Buddhists and has great influence throughout the world. Qieci, can you begin the campaign to reach the Dalai Lama. I think he will be easier to reach than the Pope, as there are much less historical and political barriers for him to speak out than for the Pope."

The conference continued with other assignments given to reach influential Christian, Jewish, Muslim, and Hindu leaders along with entertainers, politicians and other celebrities throughout the world. In North Korea, no longer under the Kim family dynasty, but still oppressed under reclusive military rule it is punishable by death to own personal computers or smart phones. It was decided to reach out to the general population through dreams from relatives in the spirit world. The citizens in China were less sheltered and there was a growing awareness of the shows and also our Internet site. Although the Politburo and its Standing Committee of China tried to restrict access to RebirthInSpirit. org there was an expanding number of enterprising young Chinese who had found ways around any blocked access. For this atheistic communist government, who had reluctantly allowed some state controlled Christian churches and Buddhist temples to exist, there was great concern over mass acceptance of the message that there is a God and that there is eternal life which would undermine the foundation of materialistic Marxism. At this time there would not be a direct campaign in China, knowing that the indirect route was already having a destabilizing effect on the totalitarian hold from the government.

We finished the conference in a high atmosphere of dedication and enthusiasm for how the work was advancing. We all knew the next steps and were motivated.

Chapter 11
Preecha Willapana

The Thai Buddhist Monk

Preecha Willapana, a short round man with a large head and lopsided smile, from Nong Khai, Thailand had reached the level of a Maha-Thera Buddhist Monk, a monk who has been in the order of Theravada Buddhism for more than twenty years, and was an administrator of the local temple. He was known to be extremely devout and doctrinal in his discipline, and towards the local populace was passionately involved in the community and with local families. To Willapana, Buddhism was the answer to everything. As the third son in a family of seven children he had been given to the Wat Lam Duan Temple at a tender age of eight to become a monk representing an offering for the family.

In Theravada Buddhism there is no concept or belief in God or a supreme being[6], so when the Thai show had Qieci, a renowned Buddhist in China who lived over a thousand years ago, talking about a loving God, Willapana found this very disturbing. He had watched all the shows that New Shambles had sponsored, plus the show in India, with growing fascination, but when the show in Thailand aired, his faith in Buddhism was shaken. Publically he stated that Buddhism was the only truth and denounced the whole expanding talk of the spirit world and belief in God, but inwardly he felt there was some truth there. For the sake of Buddhism, which had brought much good to the world for over 2,500 years, he felt compelled to make the ultimate statement.

On January 1st, 2022, Preecha Willapana set himself on fire in front of the Wat Lam Duan Temple on the shore of the Maekong River with local television stations filming the protest. This became world news and soon a documentary was made about Preecha Willapana and the conflict he had with the new revelation of spirit world.

Qieci, Martha and I, along with members of Willapana's family in the spirit world were at the temple, though of course, invisible to everyone present in their physical bodies, when Willapana died. We were notified of his impending death by thought that came from the network that keeps track of imminent passings. Good spirit world is very organized and many feel called to the ministry of informing loved ones or other interested parties that have a connection to any person on the verge of leaving their earthly life. After Willapana had his life review as all in the higher realms experience on passing over, his father and two of his sisters who had preceded him into this realm greeted and tried to comfort him.

We did not approach him at this time because his heart was still in turmoil from his violent death and we felt it best to bring him to a recovery room in a mainly Thai part of the spirit world where he would be tended over by loving people until he was ready to begin his new life. We are most comfortable among people or nations we lived with on Earth and although this is heaven without borders and anyone can travel anywhere we are drawn to places like our home areas, so above each nation on Earth is all levels of spirit world that reflect that part of Earth. So there is a Thai deep hell, a Thai hell, a Thai dark gray area, a Thai gray area, a Thai summerland, a Thai paradise, and a Thai heaven. I have heard that in the highest two realms there is no such cultural identities but rather all people share the realm together. Someday I will reside there.

Everyone's crossing into the spirit realm is unique. For those who will end up in dark areas they may be alive on Earth one day, pass on and then wake up in a hideous place with no one greeting them, since they did not love anyone while on Earth. Some don't realize they died for perhaps hundreds of years and later wonder why other people are living in their homes. These resentful Earth-bond spirits may haunt their former dwellings, becoming ghosts or even poltergeist.

For those who lived lives with love and forgiveness they would always have a life review where everything they ever did, everyone they hurt or helped intentionally or not would be revealed to them while they were surrounded by the overwhelming presence of love from God. It is not a judgment from God and the review is only for our benefit so we know what we learned and what we need to work on, who we need to approach whether they are on the Earth still or already in the spirit realms to forgive or seek forgiveness and to finally love unconditionally.

For those who die a sudden death, especially a violent death, they may need to be placed in a hall of healing, similar to a hospital. There are people who feel called to this type of work and who have been trained in the spirit world on how to send healing thoughts and love to those in their care. Also a healing light from higher realms is constantly bathing these halls of rejuvenation.

No one is required to perform any particular occupation, but we naturally gravitate to one way of helping others or another. Most in the higher realms are involved in dozens of pastimes from their main work to engaging in pleasurable entertainment, such as; creating or experiencing art or music, sailing on boats, driving their cars as we saw earlier with the Andersons, exploring different cultures that reside in this level or even exploring other solar systems, other planets throughout the galaxy or even beyond the milky way visiting other intelligent and spiritual life forms from other systems. We are free to do our main job when we wish and also other pastimes or we can end one type of work and start another. With millions in these realms there is always someone doing the necessary jobs.

Preecha Willapana's death was not a shock to him as he was the one responsible, but he definitely needed time to recuperate. We were told that in his case it would be about two or three months in Earth time before he would wake up and be ready for visitors and that a thought would come to us when he was ready.

Martha and I were taking a break out on a friend's ship in the ocean, yes there are oceans and lakes, rivers, mountains and valleys here, more beautiful than anyone on Earth can even imagine, when we got the thought that Willapana was waking. Qieci had been in the predominantly Chinese section working on perfecting dim sum cooking and we all immediately arrived outside the hall of healing, greeted each other and walked into the hall and towards Willapana's bed. We were warmly welcomed and greeted by attendants and then were left alone for privacy.

Qieci approached and sat on the bed next to the sleeping figure and when Willapana opened his eyes, he said, "Hello Preecha, do you know where you are?"

Willapana responded cautiously, "Well, I remember lighting myself on fire, and then so much pain, and then the pain was gone and I saw my Father and my two sisters who died before I did. So I guess I must also be dead. And I recognize you from that TV show where you were speaking from the other side." Then pausing with a dreadful look proclaimed, "Oh my! Then it's all true! I'm so very sorry that I took my life; that I couldn't accept this new truth. How did I end up in such a beautiful place since I killed myself?" Willapana wept out loud in anguish.

Martha and I stepped forward so he could see us also and Martha said, "Preecha you lived a life of love and sacrifice. You always served everyone you met and cared for all people. You took your life not out of a selfish reason, but because your belief in Buddhism was your whole universe. We are sorry that we brought doubt in your life, but it is time for all of God's children to know of his love. There will be a lot of pain and confusion during this time of transition, but that will pass as more people realize the simplicity of God's desire for us. He wants us to be free, free from false concepts, free from ignorance, free from small minded-ness, from pain and hatred and most of all, free to know God's love. God began Buddhism, even though it didn't recognize or honor him. It was right for the people at that time and place. God initiated all the religions and they have helped to elevate mankind spiritually, but they all had one purpose and that was to prepare us for the time when we could know God. We are at the beginning of that new age."

"I recognize you and this man. He is your husband, right? I saw you on that website where you were on the TV show in America, the one that started this whole mess from spirit world," Willapana said.

"Yes," I chuckled, "I am Dan and this is my wife, Martha and we were asked to start this whole mess. And you are now a resident of the Spirit World. When you are ready we would like to show you around."

Willapana was a very good man with the innocence of a child. He soaked up all that we taught him and soon loved his life here. When he was ready we brought him to Rajinda who wanted to mentor him and prepare him to help us in our work. His face had been broadcast throughout the world and we needed to move quickly while people still remembered that crazy Buddhist monk who had killed himself defend-ing his beliefs. There could be no greater proof of the spirit world than someone known the world over, someone the world had watched die, then there was the documentary on his life and finally to be addressing the world from the spirit side. New Shambles was planning a show for April in Estonia and we wanted Willapana to be on that show. It didn't matter that Estonia was not a Buddhist country for more and more peo-ple were watching all the shows available on RebirthInSpirit.org from all over the world. New Shambles paid the Thai company that made the documentary and the original Thai TV station that had filmed his death for the right to put these on the website right after the Estonia show.

While waiting for the Estonia show there were groups beginning to form in nations throughout the world, people who were embracing our message. Some groups in naming their organization used the name Shambles in creative ways, like; "Old Shambles, New Hope; Shambles No More; or Lovin' Shambles." The message of loving God and loving people was transforming lives. Some people finally felt free of dogma, free of the fear of death and of the unknown, free of a judgmental God, free to love life. Of course in the whole world population this was a minority, but a growing and increasingly vocal minority.

The Estonia Show

Estonia has a football stadium, the Kalevi Keskstaadion, in the city of Tallinn with a capacity of 12,000. New Shambles negotiated to rent the stadium for Saturday, April 9, 2022. There are enormous screens around the stadium so everyone can see whatever is broadcast like they were watching in a theater. With an entrance fee of 20 Euros the stadium sold out within a week of posting on RebirthinSpirit.org. With the site so popular New Shambles found they did not need to advertise on other venues for any of their events. By tracking the sign ups they could see that the majority of the attendees were coming from northern Europe, but also from Russia, Norway, Finland, Sweden with a few even from the United States.

It was decided that Martha and I would again be the spirit hosts along with Qieci translating, as the main show would be interviewing Preecha Willapana. Mike Templeton and Jackie Nagorski had built up a following from their several shows together and were briefed about what the show would be about. On the Estonian television station, Eesti Televisioon, were co-hosts Georg Kruus and Elif Vaher showcasing a popular talk show, Tänases Maailmas (The World Today), with a live audience. They were excited to be part of this spiritual movement sweeping the globe and both were fluent in English the chosen language for our show and the most universal language.

April 9 turned out to be a cloudy day with temperatures reaching 42° F but heading towards freezing as the 8 p.m. show neared. Mike and Jackie were well bundled up coming from a much warmer California the day before. Fortunately there was no rain or snow forecast for the day or it might have been quite miserable in the open stadium. For the

Estonians they took the weather in stride as this was normal for this time of the year and they were glad that the long winter was coming closer to the end.

Georg and Elif were rosy cheeked and laughing as the director gave them the countdown, 7 – 6 – 5 – 4 with the last three only with fingers counting 3 – 2 –1. "Good evening and welcome to the first worldwide showing of Tänases Maailmas, which means The World Today to our English speaking audience. This is also our first show in an outdoor stadium instead of our studio, with over 12,000 here and another 500 in the Estonia Concert Hall," Georg said.

Elif continued, "We would like to welcome world-renown New Shambles hosts, Mike Templeton and Jackie Nagorski to our humble country." A boisterous cheer rose from the crowd. "Not the same as warm California where it is summer all year long, is it?"

Jackie laughed and replied, "Thank you for such a heartfelt welcome and though we have chilly days this is much colder than is healthy for spoiled Californians unless we are skiing in the mountains."

Mike added, "It is great to be here but I think my ears are going to fall off."

Georg put in, "Please let our audience know what they are going to see today. Your shows have been incredible and I believe the impact, along with your website, are shaking a lot of people up. Elif and I are very much into shaking people up, as that is our modus operandi. Isn't that right, Elif?" Elif blew him a kiss and smiled.

Jackie responded, "Well we will have the original guests from the spirit world, Dan and Martha Everheart who were on The Tammy Show and the ancient Chinese guest, Qieci, along with a surprise guest. Are we ready to welcome our otherworldly guests?" The director nodded and the big screens came alive with Martha and me taking up half the screen with the Earthly representatives taking up the other half.

Mike was clapping and welcomed us, "Hey Dan and Martha, long time since we have seen you two. Welcome to this frozen world of Estonia!"

I laughed and said, "We never heard of Estonia in our Earthly lives, but I can see you are a hearty and happy people. We were listening in before the video went live and like you from California, in the spirit realms we are used to a sunny warm environment, in fact that is all we ever feel in the higher realms."

Martha, sitting next to me, reached out and held my arm, and added, "We so hope that as many people as possible can join us here when your life on Earth is done. That is our whole purpose of reaching out to the physical world at this time, to give you hope, and to give you simple instructions, to love others and to love God. Don't get bogged down with rules and strictures on how to live and what to believe in. Today we are showing up in our usual spirit dress for the first time. You can see they are shimmering white robes with different colors dancing in the white and with a different color belt holding them together. You can't see all the colors that are here in the spirit world but I think you get the idea."

Georg said, "Thank you Dan and Martha for honoring us with your presence on our show. You probably don't know that Estonia is considered the least religious country in the world, so in that it is an ideal place for your message. We are not bogged down at all with religious thinking," and he laughed and Elif laughed with him.

Elif added with mischief in her eyes, "Some countries have tried to impose their religions on us, but we kicked them out long ago. But I love your robes, maybe I can start a new fashion brand, how about calling it, Rüüdes Vaim." The crowd cheered. "That means Spirit Robes," she added.

Jackie interjected, "I also love your gowns. Elif, can I join you in your venture?"

Elif laughed, "Sure sister, let's talk after the show."

I said, "Thank you for your welcome. We want to bring in Qieci who was on the show in Thailand and who will be translating for our special guest. Qieci come on in. Qieci came in wearing a similar robe with a belt of gold and blue. Qieci said, "Thank you for having me join you. It is getting rather crowded with four on Earth and now three in spirit. We have one more person to add, who is a new comer to our world. You remember when the show in Thailand was aired there were some protests going on, and especially focused on one Buddhist monk, who chose a very catastrophic way of protesting. He set himself on fire." There was a gasp and a hush fell over the audience for everyone knew of this event. "Preecha Willapana please come out and greet the Earth one more time."

Preecha Willapana came into the spirit room and bowed. "Oh my God," said Elif, obviously also astonished at who the surprise guest was.

He was not wearing the spirit robe the others had on, but rather his Earthly Buddhist monk robe. "Thank you, I speak in Thai, is OK?" he said.

The screens showed only Qieci and Willapana now. Qieci said, "We will have Preecha tell his story now and I will translate along with subtitles below." Qieci spoke to Willapana in Thai and as Willapana replied some tears came to his eyes.

Qieci then addressed the audience; "I am a simple monk who loves Buddhism to my very soul. When I saw these shows on the spirit world I became upset to see people from many different religions. In Buddhism we do not believe in God but we do honor our ancestors who died before us, so you can say we have some belief in spirit world. But it was so confusing. I love my community, my neighbors, many families and they were coming to me asking me so many questions."

There was more exchange between Qieci and Willapana and Qieci continued, "Finally I want to help my Buddhist community, to keep their belief, and so I decided I had to make a statement. When the show came to my country, Thailand, I knew it was time. I remembered during the Viet Nam war and during other conflicts other Buddhist monks set themselves on fire as an ultimate statement. I decided to do the same outside the studio where this show on spirit world was going on."

The translation continued, "Well, when I died at first I saw my Father and my two sisters and then I was put in a place to rest for a long time and when I awoke I saw Qieci and this couple, Daniel and Martha."

Qieci explained, "Depending on how a person crosses over into the spirit realms his spirit may need some rest and healing of their soul. To die with anguish in his soul and in such a horrific way, Preecha needed a couple months of Earth time to recuperate. We have special places of rest for this purpose. Dan, Martha and I were there when Preecha passed though he didn't see us then but as is customary he saw people who know him and love him first and then we brought him to our realm. We knew that with so much world news about this monk, how he died and why, that he could be very important to our message to the world."

Willapana and Qieci spoke together and Willapana started to cry. Qieci said, "Preecha woke up and was so surprised to see it was all true, all that the shows had revealed. He felt so ashamed and did not know why he was in such a good place, since he had believed in different things and had died by his own hands. He said he met people who only had love for him, so much love, and most were not Buddhists."

Qieci continued after talking with Willapana, "After staying with Dan and Martha for a while and learning more about this new world I was brought to an even higher realm where Garuda and Rajinda live, remember they were the couple hosting the show in India. A messenger from that realm came and placed her hands on my head and did something that allowed me to go to a higher heaven, otherwise I would not have been able to breathe there. If you think the realm you have seen with Dan and Martha is amazing, you would not believe what it is like in the higher realms. So beautiful! So beautiful!"

Qieci added, "I am afraid your technology can't do any justice to the higher realms. It would be a mistake if we were to try to show you, you would not be able to perceive most of it. Everything in the higher realms of spirit world is alive, the ground, the air, the water in oceans and rivers. Everything responds to humans, especially to our love and appreciation. Only in these realms can you begin to understand how much God truly loves us, it is forever overwhelming and magnificent. Also there is no end to how much you can grow to higher and higher levels, even beyond what are known as the divine or celestial levels."

Qieci spoke to Willapana for a while and then addressed the viewers, "Rajinda changed my heart and allowed me to grow much more than I thought possible. Her love and vision is incredible. She showed me how I could help people so much more because I had become so well known on Earth. I didn't know that they had me on all those news shows and even told my story on a TV documentary seen all over the world. So now I could be a real story, alive on the Earth, everyone saw me die and now to be able to speak to you from here. I am so grateful, so very grateful, that my life and death were not a waste. Can you understand what this means to me?"

The large screens were once again showing the Earth side hosts and guests. Elif had tears flowing down her cheeks and Georg was also visibly moved. Mike was slowly rocking back and forth and Jackie was smiling.

The cameras in the spirit realm also pulled back and Martha and I were shown coming over and placing our hands over Willapana and a blue healing light was coming from our hands showering over him. Qieci joined us in this healing love and Willapana was crying with gratitude.

I said, "Martha and I were Christians, Rajinda was Hindu, Qieci and Preecha were Buddhists. But it is not the religion that is important, but that you live your lives with love and compassion. Preecha died by suicide and I want to strongly warn against taking your own life. He was very fortunate to be such a good and loving person and did not take his life as a means to escape his hardships but because he loved his religion so much. Religions are a gift from God to help us in our lives. If you are part of a religion, that is good, and I encourage you to become the best Christian, Buddhist, Muslim, Hindu or whatever. But also love and respect all other religions and their followers. They are all teaching the same things, fundamentally. We hope this show was a gift to everyone watching." Smiling Martha and I waved goodbye. Qieci bowed his head with his hands clasped together.

Willapana turned and faced the cameras and said in English, "Thank you for hearing me. I love all of you. Thank you."

The spirit side cameras went dark and the screens then only showed the Earth side presenters. Mike said, "Man, what a tearjerker. I didn't know that this would be so powerful." The cameras were scanning the crowd showing people with tears flowing, others with stunned faces, some were hugging people close to them.

Georg said, "Well, after this maybe Estonia will no longer be known as the least religious place on Earth."

Elif wiping her eyes said, "Amen to that." And everyone laughed.

Chapter 12
Samuel

Second Visit with Samuel

Martha came to me after the Estonia Show her eyes bright and intense. "Samuel has been thinking about what we told him. I can feel him searching in his heart, remembering some tender times we shared together when he was young," Martha said. "I want to go see him again."

"Should I come also?" I asked. "Yes, please come every time so he can see you care for him, whether or not he is willing to speak with you or not. Jerry should come also because Sam respects him when he was so quick to jump in to defend me the first time," Martha added.

We sent a thought to Jerry and he was eager to come with us. A moment later he was standing with us ready to go. I walked over and gave him a hug, "Thanks for helping with our son," I said. Jerry smiled saying, "Sure, he's my brother and I love you guys."

We concentrated on Samuel and entered his hell once again, the air black and heavy. This time Sam felt our presence and coming out of a cave stepped over a couple of filthy women crawling in the mud. They were revolting hags with sores all over them. One looked at me and screamed, "It's not my fault! She was dead already!" Sam kicked her in the side and spat out, "Shut up witch, no one cares." I winched at his cruelty but did not let my revulsion show in my face.

Martha reached out to him but he backed away. Jerry said, "Come on Sam, we are here to help you." Samuel looked at Jerry and his anger softened a little. I leaned on a rock covered with scum saying nothing, ready to engage if allowed. Two of Sam's henchmen were standing near, hulking beasts with killing in their bloodshot eyes.

Samuel motioned us into his cave, and though he still looked at me with gut gripping resentment allowed me to follow. "Don't let any assholes bother us," Sam hissed at the goons and they closed ranks over the entrance.

I listened in and after a while heard Martha saying, "You have to ask God to forgive you. He surely will if you are sincere. You don't have to live in this filth. You aren't condemned for eternity, when you look for God he will be there." We were there for some time and I could feel the atmosphere lighten slightly.

When we left I could see tears in Samuel's eyes.

Chapter 13
North Korea

The North Korea Campaign

North Korea is the most oppressive country in the world. It is illegal to privately own a cell phone unless authorized by the government; all televisions can only receive the government stations that are full of propaganda extolling the greatness of the Republic of Korea and the evils of other countries, with America the worst enemy. The people are told that their country is the most prosperous and advanced in the world, even though there is massive hunger and lack of even the basic needs for life. The people of North Korea were not aware of any of the programs that had been aired from the spirit world or of the website answering questions that people have had for thousands of years. They were a nation removed, cut off from the world.

Before the communists took over the country north of the demilitarized zone Korea was one nation, predominantly a Buddhist country but also with a growing and fervent Christian faith. Pyongyang, the capital of North Korea, had been known as the Jerusalem of Asia with small Christian churches blossoming on almost every corner. With the advancement of atheistic communism dividing the nation, most of the pastors in the North were killed or sent to reeducation hard labor camps. Thousands of pastors and congregants perished in these death camps.

There are still many people in North Korea who remember Korea when it was one nation, a nation of zealous faith. No matter how much the government tried to suppress any religious belief the underground churches still existed. But as the population ages the faithful are dying off and hopelessness is taking its place. We were very aware of this dark country.

There had been a very concerted effort from the higher realms of the spirit world to combat atheistic communism during the Soviet Union's expansion of Marxism throughout the world. This was a very real good-versus-evil war in the world and in the spirit world. Powerful dark and evil spirits were influencing susceptible people to deny the existence of God and even deny the very spirit world they were working from and to embrace dialectical materialism instead. From the higher realms of the spirit world where we lived in the love of God, there was a huge effort to keep faith alive in these countries under attack. That effort is continuing in China, Cuba and other oppressed countries giving fire and inspiration to the underground faith movements.

No matter how much these countries tried they could not eliminate the underground churches and finally had to allow some government sanctioned churches where all sermons were monitored and messages were controlled. Regardless, the underground churches were still growing. But in North Korea it was different. The brainwashing control and oppression were near complete.

Despite how powerful the government was they had no control over our spiritual infiltration. With the level of belief so strong when North Korea was part of a free nation and the faith in South Korea still growing there were now several million Koreans in higher spirit world dwelling in a majority Korean area (remember, we dwell where we are most comfortable, even in heaven).

Garuda and Rajinda had some meetings with people of Korean ancestry in their own higher realm on creating a strategy to reach the lost people of North Korea. For those still concerned with what was happening on Earth, they began a very organized effort to rain down through dreams and inspirations focusing on the people still living in this isolated country. The message, though unique and personal for each person, was basically the same. There is a God, there is eternal life and hope and liberation is coming.

Oppression is maintained through fear, fear of neighbors who will inform on you, fear of your own children who are taught in school to inform of any anti-government words or actions of their parents, fear that any action no matter how small can result in you being arrested and sent to a hard labor camp along with everyone in your family. These camps are full of regular citizens starving and being worked to death where guards have absolute authority to abuse you or end your life for any reason.

The suffering of these millions of people was strongly felt by concerned people in our realms and especially was felt by God. People who are suffering because of ignorance and improper action are not as heart wrenching as people who are suffering from total hopelessness. We therefore had to give them hope, to be a spark of light in this heavy darkness.

Through dreams people were told whom they could trust, who was also having similar dreams or who already had some understanding of God and eternal life. They were also told who not to trust, who might seem friendly, but would not hesitate to denounce them and therefore gain some benefits for turning in a "traitor." Every person on Earth has to sleep, usually at night, and that was our time to work.

It was this population that we were reaching and our influence was growing. When the fear of what comes after death is removed then the threat of death has no more power over people. Even the threat of death to your son or daughter or wife or husband or father or mother or anyone you love loses its effective power when you realize they will be freed in the ending of their life. When the government loses this coercive control they have truly lost. It becomes a formidable force when the population of a nation has nothing to fear. Nothing can stop this force.

For a closed society this was our way to reach out, slow but effective, until the regime is shut down and light flows into the nation.

Chapter 14

The Popes

The Pope Question

There is no organization on the Earth like the Catholic Church, where one man is respected by over a billion people, and for most adherents of the Roman Catholic Church whatever the Pope says is the word of God without the possibility of error. The belief in the infallibility of the Pope remains a potent power even though three recent Popes distanced themselves from infallibility.

In July 2005 Pope Benedict XVI stated during an impromptu address to priests that: "The Pope is not an oracle; he is infallible in very rare situations, as we know." His predecessor Pope John XXIII once remarked: "I am only infallible if I speak infallibly but I shall never do that, so I am not infallible."[7] On the issue of homosexuality Pope Francis stated, "…who am I to judge?"[8] astonishing Catholics everywhere who might have asked, "if not you, then who?"

The current Pope, the first Asian Bishop of Rome, Agus Yulianto from Indonesia, who chose the name Pope Matthew V, was hesitant toward restoring the belief in infallibility, in his own infallibility. Pope Matthew, at 5 foot 5 inches, handsome with Indonesian features at 64, was a good man, humble and sincere, and sensitive to spirit world influences.

Our former Catholic priest in Jiva Satata, Sean McCoy, had thoroughly researched the history of Papal authority in the Hall of Knowledge to find the Popes who were the 'good ones' and who would be appropriate to help in this operation. He decided on three: St. Gregory I (Gregorius; 590-604), Pius IX (Giovanni Maria Mastai-Ferretti; 1846-78)[9] and Pope John Paul II (Karol Józef Wojtyla;1978-2005). With permission from the highest realms he sent out thoughts to Gregorius, Giovanni Mastai-Ferretti and Karol Wojtyla, to meet for a very important mission.

On what would be June 20, 2022 in Earth time the three men, dressed in their spirit robes, appeared outside Sean McCoy's home and walked up to the front door. "Welcome friends to my home. Please make yourselves comfortable. Before I start, how would you like to be addressed, considering your former positions and mine in the Roman Catholic Church?" Sean asked as he brought out refreshments for his guests.

"We three are well acquainted and are good friends having shared the same burden of authority. Just call us by our first names and you

one of us to lead them astray. I agree with Karol that if the Pope and those who advise him were given a consistent vision of Mary they might be persuaded. But still no matter what, they will never be willing to just dump everything the church is and what it believes in for a vague belief in a heaven for anyone, believer or not, and for a non-permanent hell that the worst sinner, the most evil person can work their way out of and into heaven. You may have to approach the Catholic population worldwide from the bottom up rather than try to convince the Pope and leadership to lead the way. This is sad, but I think there is too much at stake for the Pope, even if it is the will of God."

Sean sighed and said, "You may be right, I will report all of this to Garuda and Rajinda and I am sure they will bring the recommendation of visitations from Mary even higher for consideration. I appreciate all your contributions."

Karol said, "I think I speak for my friends, but we would very much like to join your group and be a part of this effort."

Sean looked around at these three noble men and said, "We will be honored to have you with us. Thank you. And thank you for your valuable advice."

Chapter 15

The World Responds

Dividing the Sheep from the Goats

In Japan a group was formed called Spirit Bound that embraced the simplified idea of loving God and loving people. A former Christian non-denominational pastor, Rev. Osamu Shigiyama, was frustrated by the Christian belief that only those who believed in Jesus would be saved. Japan is less than one percent Christian, mostly being a Shinto and Buddhist nation and this narrow view of salvation kept his church stagnant. He was greatly relieved to be hearing the message from the spirit world that heaven is not reserved for Christians, but rather is for all who have nourished a heavenly nature. He formed Spirit Bound with some of his former congregants, who all still love Jesus, emphasizing a life of service and love. Without the overriding condemnation for unbelievers but instead viewing all people as brothers and sisters he found his new church was growing faster than before.

In South Korea there are several organizations that help escaped North Koreans to assimilate into their new country, helping them to find jobs and lodging and especially to understand the culture of freedom and prosperity. It is an uphill battle for most to rid themselves of fear and betrayal that permeates the North. In the widely read and influential daily South Korean newspaper, Chosun Ilbo, there was a front page article about a new phenomenon happening throughout the North, as reported by a surge of escapees. People were having vivid dreams and visitations from relatives who had passed away or ancestors telling them about God, that God is real, that he loves them and that they will live forever in the spirit world, exhorting them to live good lives.

In Britain and other parts of Europe along with many of the New England states of America the Spiritualist Churches and the Swedenborgian Churches saw a rapid growth in adherents and in curious visitors. Talk of Summerland, a Spiritualist's word for heaven, was thrown around the web and on chat sites. Through mediums of the past and present, various spirits have described heaven as a place of continual sunshine with elaborate gardens with flowers of all types in constant bloom. These descriptions are accurate of perpetual sunshine and of a profusion of gardens. These gardens in heaven, created by spirits who love horticulture, are gifts for all the homes of every person and for the public areas in their level of spirit world.[10] Like our website, Rebirthinspirit.org, Swedenborg emphasized to be careful when involved in spirit communication and only with the guidance of the Lord through sincere prayer.

Rebirthinspirit.org grew to over a billion views a day. The staff for the site had grown quickly and now was over a thousand with offices in twelve different countries, along with a dedicated staff of several hundred in the spirit lands creating videos and answering the hundreds of unique questions a day. The FAQ (Frequently Asked Questions) section was nicely divided in sub-sections, such as; What is the Nature of God?, What Happens When We Die?, How Do We Progress in Spirit?, What Should Be the Focus of Our Life on Earth?, Where Do Atheists Go in the Spirit World?, and so many more broad sections, with most also sub-sub divided narrowing down the inquiries.

One of the popular destinations on Rebirthinspirit.org was the video of when our new building, Nexus Magna, was created. Five master architects first created a blueprint of the ideas, and when approved they included the glass workers, for standard windows and stained glass, and three landscapers to envision the garden and artists trained in colorizing a public building. They had a master door maker design the front door and all other doors inside the building. All told there were about twenty five people involved. When everyone was in agreement and knew exactly the size and shape, along with all the rooms, their dimensions and where the doors and windows would be they all gathered and with focused thought concentrated on where the building would be. A huge bright light came down from a higher sphere fusing with the light coming from all the designers and the building first became a transparent vision then started solidifying into a solid structure, until it was finally as real and substantial as any other building. The gardens were added along with the paths through the different parts of the garden. The building was near the Hall of Knowledge and they complimented each other. The Hall of Knowledge, though created hundreds of years ago looked just as new and fresh as the new building, Nexus Magna.

The United Nations' Alliance of Civilizations held its 15th Global Forum in Bali, Indonesia in August 2022, with the main focus on how countries could use the spirit world message of inclusiveness to counter religious zealotry that was threatening explosive violence in the Mid-East, Africa, parts of South Asia and several nations in South America. The Alliance recognizes religions and the part they can play in advancing peace especially with inter-religious dialogue and interaction, along with other forces of culture, such as; sports, entertainment, music, art, social media and cultural exchanges.

In the United States there was a distinctive split between those who embrace the new message and those who oppose or denounce it. A charismatic Indiana pastor of the Madison Assembly of God Church, Rev. Jack Demston, called for a coalition of Christians who see the new message from the Spirit World as coming in the spirit of the anti-Christ. He appeared on the Today Show, Good Morning America, along with the Christian Television Network, the Trinity Broadcasting Network and Daystar Television.

At the same time the United Religions Initiative, based in San Francisco, but working throughout the world to further inter-religious dialogue, began sponsoring marches in major cities; Los Angeles, New York, Seoul, Rio De Janeiro, Budapest, Prague and Kiev to promote the belief that there is one God and that all faiths were relevant and important. The Universal Peace Federation, with the motto of "One World Under God" held World Summits to promote the spirit world assertions that all people were sons and daughters of God and that family was the first school for every child to learn of love, inclusiveness, compassion and belief in God. UPF sees itself as the United Nations for religions seeking faith based solutions with input from religious leaders and adherents of all the major religions to the world's divisions and struggles.

The populations of the world were reaching the point where almost everyone heard of this new phenomenon and had to choose to believe in a benevolent, non-judgmental God who did not favor any religion or belief, or to stubbornly continue in their previous belief system.

Chapter 16
Harvard

Harvard Divinity School Symposium

Harvard Divinity School was the first non-denominational divinity school in the United States created as a separate college of Harvard University in 1816. Unofficially it was connected to the Unitarian Church with historical ties to the United Church of Christ, which evolved from one of the first churches in America, the Congregation Church. Today the school is inter-religious welcoming Christian (all denominations), Jewish, Muslim, Hindu, Buddhist, Sikh, etc. who are interested in going into ministry.[11]

The dean of Harvard Divinity School, Dr. Theodore Del Torre, tall, distinguished with short brown hair and wire frame glasses, solicited Jackie Nagorski of New Shambles on the possibility of having a seminar with the theme "The Nature of God and What to Expect on Our Passing" inviting whomever we felt was appropriate from our spirit side. Jackie and all the staff at New Shambles had been instructed that whenever they needed to contact us to give a very specific thought directed to whomever they wanted to reach. Thought is powerful, both on Earth and in the spirit world. In the future people on Earth will realize they will be able to do amazing things by thought and that realization will come when they have a clearer relationship with God. For us, Jackie's thought message was very similar to any thought communication coming from someone else in our realm. Immediately we transported to Nexus Magna, our hall for communicating with the Earth and came on Jackie's computer monitor.

Martha and I were both aware of Harvard College which began in 1636, from our life in early America and knew that it had later become Harvard University. When told of the non-denominational and now inter-religious nature of Harvard Divinity School and the worldwide respect the school held we were excited to be part of this platform. We wanted it to be broadcast on as many television stations, cable and other formats as possible. We were also delighted with this request from such an educated person from such an esteemed institution and saw this as a turning point of acceptance to our message. We had not approached the college, rather Dr. Del Torre had approached New Shambles and asked them to supply guests from the spirit world, thereby showing a belief in our presentations.

We agreed to the show with the stipulation that this not be a debate between us and scholars on Earth who think they know who God is or what they think passing from the physical life to the eternal spirit life entails. There was already enough damage from theologians through the centuries putting God in a box and changing "truth" to fit their concepts.

Dr. Henry Ware was one of the instrumental men in creating Harvard Divinity School in 1816 [12] and so he was our first choice to be one of the spirit side presenters. He would represent the liberal side of Christianity, as a Unitarian Theologian.[13] There was a painting of his likeness at the school which would make it that much more intriguing to the school and the viewers. Jackie would make sure that the painting would be shown during the broadcast.

Representing more conservative and evangelical Christianity, we selected Rev. George Whitefield, a British preacher, who was one of the founders of Methodism and who preached in every colony in America in the 18th century helping to initiate the First Great Awakening in America and England.[14] I approached Mr. Ware and Mr. Whitefield and invited them to our home. They were astonished and excited by the invitation to be on a show broadcasted on Earth.

Martha and I would also be the experienced hosts from Jiva Satata coming from a Christian background and also with extensive experience on helping new arrivals to these realms. With that background we would be a great asset in addressing the second part of the theme, "What to Expect on Our Passing."

Jackie Nagorski informed Dr. Del Torre of our willingness to have this seminar and who the spirit side guests would be. He was very excited with these distinguished and historical personages and agreed to our non-debating format; especially since our spirit world guests already represent two very different sides of Christianity.

Jackie sent out press releases to the major television stations along with the Cable giants, HBO and Showtime. HBO won the bid for the show and it was decided that the original show would be a 90 minute telecast on Thanksgiving, November 24th, 2022. This was to our liking with the important holiday, the second anniversary of our initial meeting, and, as we were told, with HBO there would be no commercial interruptions, a concept that Jackie had to explain to us. Later the show would be broadcast internationally to twelve nations with a strong Christian base and more if it proved to be popular.

On November 5th, the New Shambles' and HBO's film crews arrived at Andover Hall at Harvard Divinity School and set up their equipment in the Sperry Room, a lecture hall that would be the venue for the show. The audience was invitation only with major religious leaders, theologians, professors and clergy making up the majority of the 120 guests. After editing, the show would be broadcast on Thanksgiving for the American audience. Promotions for the show were already showing up on HBO's calendar of future shows and later after the filming there would be video extractions added to the promos.

Dr. Theodore Del Torre approached the podium as the lights dimmed for the show. He had been encouraged to ask questions to the hosts and after the main presentation to take a few questions from the audience. We wanted this to be an open forum, unscripted and natural. On the dais were New Shambles' popular hosts, Jackie and Michael, with a large screen behind the platform for the spirit world hosts to make our appearance. On the podium HBO had placed the HBO logo along with the theme of the program, "A Spirit World View of the Nature of God and Life After Death," wording HBO thought would be more stimulating.

"Welcome, my friends, esteemed colleagues and leading religious thinkers of this great nation." There was both polite and enthusiastic applause from different parts of the audience. "We have all been shaken out of our comfortable lives and challenged in ways we never expected and from a source we certainly never expected. I know everyone here is aware of the broadcasts that claim to be from the next world. Whether or not you are willing to believe this source is really from heaven, you are in for a stimulating evening," Dr. Del Torre began.

"The Tammy Show in 2021 first declared the opening of communication from heaven. I didn't see that show live, I don't usually watch that kind of TV show." There was some laughter in the audience. "By your laughter I guess many of you also didn't see it live. But after all the news reports and with so many people talking about it, I watched the show on YouTube. I saw the Indian show and I started looking at the website, Rebirthinspirit.org. Then there was all that news about the Buddhist monk who lit himself on fire outside the show in Thailand and amazingly later, after he died, coming on the Estonia show. Well, I am stumped. Either this is a very elaborate hoax or we are living in an incredible time. Tonight I hope we find some answers. Well, I have taken up too much valuable time.

If you have been watching this whole development then you are familiar with our guests from New Shambles, Jackie Nagorski and Michael Templeton. Welcome, and please introduce what is in store for us this evening." Cordial applause followed this introduction.

Michael responded, "Thank you, Dr. Del Torre. I am really out of my league here, I am a computer engineer, I barely believed in God before all this came along. Jackie is more spiritual, so I think she should introduce our program."

Jackie chuckled and said, "We are honored to be here and are also honored to introduce our guests from the spirit world. Most of you have seen Daniel and Martha Everheart on other shows. They will be the two hosts from the spirit side and they have invited two very special guests to join us. When you arrived at Andover Hall this evening perhaps you saw the painting of one of the founders of Harvard Divinity School, Dr. Henry Ware. He will be one of our guests this evening." There were gasps from the audience. And as Jackie spoke a picture of the painting and a brief history of Dr. Ware was projected on the screen. She continued "Dr. Ware was a Unitarian theologian representing the liberal path to Christianity and to have a balanced program we also invited someone who had a tremendous impact on Britain and the American colonies, the evangelical pastor, Rev. George Whitefield, who helped initiate the First Great Awakening." The audience erupted and a lady in the audience said quite loudly, "Oh my God!" On the screen was a painting of Rev. Whitefield and a brief bio on him.

The screen faded to black and then Martha and I, dressed in our spirit robes, came on the screen. Martha said with a big smile and eyes shining, "Hello everyone on the Earth-side, once again. If you have seen our other shows then you know I am Martha Everheart and this is my husband, Daniel. We are honored to have this great opportunity to address the great religious leaders in modern America. I understand this show will be shown throughout the world also. How exciting this all is!"

I added, "As you just heard our two guests tonight are Dr. Henry Ware and Rev. George Whitefield. We never heard of our guest, Henry Ware, while we were alive. I died before he was born though my wife was still on the Earth while he was a young man. But we are very familiar with Rev. George Whitefield. In fact, we both heard Rev. Whitefield when he came to Southold on Long Island, New York in 1739. He was a powerful preacher and through him, my wife and I became Christians. Let us introduce them to you now." The camera pulled back revealing two men sitting in chairs next to us.

Martha said, "It is our honor to introduce Dr. Henry Ware, one of the founders of Harvard Divinity School in 1816 and a Unitarian theologian and minister. He lived from 1764 to 1845," and she indicated the man with dark hair and a sloping nose. Mr. Ware acknowledged the introduction with a slight bow of his head and a smile. Both guests appeared to be in their late twenties, as is the general case of most people in the spirit world. "And Rev. George Whitfield, an open air evangelical preacher, who started in the Anglican faith and later was one of the first to promote Methodism and was part of the First Great Awakening of Christian faith in America. He lived from 1714 to 1770." Martha indicated a smaller man with a round face and Mr. Whitefield, smiling, gave a little wave of his hand.

"To initiate this first discussion on What is the Nature of God I would like both of you to describe what you believed while on Earth and then how your understanding of God may have changed since coming to the spirit world," I said, "Dr. Ware, would you like to start?"

Mr. Ware looked down at his hands and smiled, "Well, first of all I want to thank Daniel and Martha here in spirit world for inviting me. I also want to acknowledge Dr. Del Torre and Jackie and Michael and the whole audience watching now and in future replaying. It is amazing to me, and overwhelming to be able to address the people on Earth and especially at my former school, Harvard Divinity School. This is remarkable. Well to your question, I was a Unitarian theologian, intellectual, reasonable and somewhat proud. As a Unitarian, I did not believe that Jesus was God, or in the trinity, that God could be separated into three parts. God was God, the creator of man, the Earth, the Universe, along with the initiator of natural laws and the sciences. God was the source of our reason and related to us through our reason along with through inspiration, or divine inspiration, if you will. God was a separate being, an observer of his creation, distant. I did not believe in any creed or in-fallible doctrine or dogma, but rather in our free will."[12]

"Let me tell you when my understanding was first really challenged," Mr. Ware continued, "and that was when I died, or passed into this next world. I felt an overwhelming love embrace me, nonjudgmental, deeply interested in me as a person, so much so, that at that moment I was the most valuable person to this God. God is such a crude word to describe our eternal parent. He was at once my father, my mother also, my clos-est friend, someone who wanted to share everything with me." As Mr. Ware was speaking tears began to flow down his cheeks. "I would have found it so demeaning to cry over something like this on Earth, like I was some emotional born-again Christian. But it is a love I feel every moment here. I realized that my arrogant intellectual understanding of a distant God was painful to God. God does not want to be glorified for his reasonableness, for his intelligence. We theologians, a word I now find offensive, believed that God was unknowable, unmovable, a mys-tery that we could never know personally. God is none of these things. God is knowable and is moved by our lives, by our efforts to grow and to learn to love as he does. I am not able to describe the love I feel coming from God." Mr. Ware spread his hands and nodded slightly, indicating that was his end of his initial statement.

Jackie was looking over the audience of important people, some self-important, others who had made some real contributions to the faith community. Some looked shocked and betrayed at such an emotional display from an intellectual giant, like Dr. Ware. Others looked fasci-nated, intrigued by such an honest openhearted beginning, dispelling any notion that this would be a dry intellectual discussion. Jackie had gone through her own spiritual transformation from an assistant pastor at an evangelical church to a lay person in a spiritualist church. She said, "Thank you, Dr. Ware, every one of us has our own search for God. It is moving to find that God is deeply concerned for each one of us; that we matter to him personally. I think many will find that challenging, that you, that I am valuable to God."

I looked over at Mr. Whitefield and asked, "Well, Rev. Whitefield, what was your belief on Earth and has there been any changes since coming to the spirit world?"

Mr. Whitefield responded first with a laugh, "I was that emotional born-again Christian, Dr. Ware referred to. I deeply loved God and Jesus while on Earth and was compelled to share wherever I went. It was recorded that I gave over 18,000 speeches during my ministry in Britain and in the colonies of this new world. People would drop everything, leave their fields, grab their families and push their horses to exhaustion to travel 20, 30 miles to hear my sermons. My sermons would be filled with thousands of people, up to 20,000 people out in the open air while I would speak from a building so they could hear me. My words were full of God's love, of Jesus dying for our sins and God's judgment, of eternal hell-fire. By the way, did you know that I was cross-eyed? Some who knew that about me might have been looking to see if I was really George Whitefield, looking at my eyes. Well, that physical imperfection did not continue into the spirit world. At the end of my talks I would always ask people to come to the front, confess their sins, and receive new life by accepting Jesus and by being reborn through the Holy Spirit. Hundreds of thousands of people came to Christ. Seven times I traveled to the colonies from England to preach, which means I crossed the Atlantic Ocean fourteen times to preach on one side or the other."[13]

"I am saying all this to show how sure I was; I was unstoppable. Imagine my surprise to come to heaven and find people like Dr. Ware here," he chuckled and glanced at Mr. Ware, "or Catholics or even Hindus, Muslims, Buddhists. It took me a long time to accept all this, and to find that God does not judge us and hell for an individual lasts only as long as someone remains unrepentant. No more eternal gnashing of teeth in a sulfur pit of fire. My understanding of God was severely challenged."

I interrupted saying, "Just for clarification and for the sake of the audience on Earth we have been using the titles you feel appropriate, such as Doctor or Reverend, but we don't use those titles here. On Earth people feel more important when given a title but here our honor is not derived by what degree at a university we have received or whether we have been ordained by a church. I assure you there are some in deep hell who had many righteous titles while on Earth, and also some in very high spirit world who never attended any school or church in their lives. Our elevation here is through our love and our active service to others."

Dr. Del Torre responded, "Well, we certainly are being challenged, whether we come from an orthodox or liberal faith, and almost everyone here has some title of importance. I guess it is like they say; you can't take it with you, your wealth, your possessions and your titles even. Dr. Ware, or Mr. Ware I should say, what do you feel you got right in your life that allowed you to be where you are today?"

Martha interjected first, "For this show please feel free to call these fine gentlemen by the titles they were known by on Earth. My husband was never a reverend so he feels strongly about this, though he can be preachy at times." As she said this she looked at me sternly and chastened, I grinned and held my hands open in defeat. There was some laughter in the audience at our interaction. "Dr. Ware, please continue," she added smiling.

"Thanks and that's a good question," Mr. Ware responded. "My desire was to help my students open their minds to seek for truth wherever that meant they had to venture. I invested in their lives and in the community around. I wanted Harvard Divinity School to be a place where people could find God, even if it challenged the beliefs they were raised on and so it was opened as the first interdenominational ministerial college in America. I admit I was helping the students find truth through an intellectual path, but it was altruistic, nonetheless. I found it is our motives that are important, do we do what we do to enhance ourselves only or are we helping others? I deeply cared for the students and for their families when I met them."

Dr. Del Torre interjected, "Rev. Whitefield," and he winked at Martha, "You seemed to have been even more challenged than Dr. Ware, when you realized the nature of spirit world and who goes where. Based on that and getting back to our theme, "What is the Nature of God," what do you now say God is like?"

"As Dr. Ware first shared he found that God is deeply interested in each person. We built the walls that keep God out, to the point where it seems God is uninvolved in our lives," Mr. Whitefield explained. "My message on Earth was repentance and to be born again and that is still my message. I am still a preacher and with others go into different parts of hell to find people who show a spark of repentance. Before I was judgmental, but now it is only out of love because that is what I have found from God, unconditional, nonjudgmental love and always overwhelming forgiveness. I obviously no longer talk about eternal damnation. But I still share of Jesus the Messiah, the Savior and of his sacrifice and example, but no longer that Jesus is God. Because I sincerely loved Jesus

I was invited and have met Jesus on several occasions and he was very grateful for my ministry. But he told me he was deeply disappointed that the majority of Christians decided to believe that he was God. That was solidified in 325 AD at the Council of Nicea where the doctrine of the trinity was formalized."

"Hold on, this is a very important point," said Dr. Del Torre, "Jesus told you that the belief in the trinity is mistaken?"

Mr. Whitefield continued, "Yes, and I argued with Jesus, if you can believe that. But he is a person, a human, like you and me. Well, not like us, he is sinless and has reached divinity, but he is not God himself. He told me when Christians put him into the Godhead they change his message. If Jesus is God, we can excuse ourselves to never live our lives like Jesus did. But we are all meant to be God's sons and God's daughters. We are all meant to live a life connected to God, where we feel God's love and presence at all times. We are all meant to and can reach divinity like Jesus did. That was the purpose of his life, to be an example, to open a pathway, to be our brother, to be our friend, not to be unreachable, distant like we have also made God, worshiped on a pedestal. But he also came as the Messiah, to be the bridge between God and man, to be the successful Adam to give us rebirth, where the first Adam failed."

"But more on the nature of God, He will not interfere with what we believe, even in the spirit world. If you can believe it, there are still churches in heaven that preach the old message of the trinity; of God the Father, God the Son and God the Holy Spirit. To make the message real to each one of us individually, we have to find God ourselves. If we ask, He will be there for us. But most often we tell God what we believe, and then He will just wait patiently for us. He has infinite patience and infinite love. One of the reasons I was chosen to come on this show is because I came to understand who Jesus really was."

Dr. Ware said, "You asked what I did right while on Earth, and I could have mentioned the belief that there was only one God, not a triune God. But it was much more valuable to come from such a powerful preacher like Rev. Whitefield."

"On our earlier shows from the spirit realms we did not address specifics from any religion, what was true or what wasn't," Martha cautiously interjected. "Since we were invited by this college we felt it was time to begin narrowing down the message. Rev. Whitefield and Dr. Ware's testimonies are extremely important to help the Christian world find their way. We don't expect the Pope, the Catholic Church or most Christian churches to readily accept what we are saying. In fact, we expect some demonstrations against our shows and probably more violence like we have already seen. Speaking of that, Mike and Jackie, how are you doing? Are you still receiving threats?"

Mike responded with a concerned look, "Yes, we are. I don't even look at my email anymore and only answer the phone when I recognize the caller through caller ID. We travel with bodyguards all the time. But you know I wouldn't have it any other way. Through my experience with you in spirit world I am not afraid to die and now have a purpose to make my life count."

Jackie added, "I agree with Mike, I feel honored to be a part of this. When death has no power you can do anything, no matter the threat."

"I don't think anyone realized how these shows have challenged your lives at New Shambles," Dr. Del Torre with all sincerity said. "I am even more honored that you came here. Thank you. The second part of our theme for the show is more general, Life After Death. We heard that Rev. Whitefield is still a preacher to lost souls, what do you do Dr. Ware, I don't know how to say this, but for lack of a better word, what is your occupation in spirit world?"

Mr. Ware responded, "We don't have occupations here, as I think you know, we don't need to eat or sleep or even need to have a home or shelter and of course there is no commerce here. But I have occupied my time with a number of pursuits, some for my own benefit, like becoming a proficient painter, and for a higher purpose I work in a hall that keeps track of people who are about to pass into the spirit world. We locate and let their loved ones know along with some select people who have been trained to educate new arrivals."

"Why don't you explain how that works," Martha said.

Mr. Ware continued, "Well for those who will go to a higher sphere, generally a close relative along with a couple of the trained people will go to Earth and be where the person is breathing his or her last breathes. They will then take the person away from the death scene and bring them to their level of spirit world where they will begin their eternal life. It will feel like they are traveling through a long tunnel at a very high speed."

"Oh, the famous tunnel with the light at the end," Dr. Del Torre put in.

"Yes, that is quite real although not like a tunnel on Earth," Mr. Ware continued. "They will actually travel through the low realms, but so rapidly the newly departed will not be able to see and be disturbed by anything they pass. In order to work where I do, I have also been trained as one who goes to Earth to assist those passing over and I have done that hundreds of times. Daniel and Martha are specially trained people who also go to Earth to welcome new arrivals and later educate them about life in the spirit world. With a person nearing their transition I send a thought to someone like Daniel and Martha, and they respond with either they are available or are otherwise occupied and to ask someone else."

"It is something we deeply enjoy, first the welcome and then the training about life in the spirit world. For many new arrivals, they have a home waiting for them, the home they would have always liked to live in," I said. "Sorry, please continue Dr. Ware."

Mr. Ware added, "Whomever the trainers that are going from spirit world, they first appear at our hall and we give them the impression, or like a living picture, and the name of the person passing. We don't have to tell them where to go, but rather the impression is like a magnetic pull that brings them to the right place on Earth every time. The loved one from spirit world of the person passing may be there before those assigned to help, and they always appreciate those who are trained to assist in the passing. It can be an extremely emotional time for the relative looking forward to welcome their loved one, so it is good to have a steadying presence there. Later when they arrive at the sphere they are going to, the person who just passed will see a review of their life, as it actually happened, who they hurt intentionally or not, who they helped, who they loved and will feel the presence of God or Jesus, or another high spirit depending on your background, not in judgment but surrounding the person in understanding and love. Then depending on how the person died, they may be put into a hall of rest for as long as needed, especially if it was a sudden or violent death, or if a more peaceful passing there might be a whole group of relatives, ancestors or friends ready to welcome their loved one. Every passing is different and may not follow this sequence exactly, but I think this gives you a good beginning."

Jackie said, "Dr. Del Torre, when you first approached us for this conference you wanted the second part of the program to tell what happens when someone passes into the spirit world. I think this has helped answer that question."

Mr. Del Torre responded, "This has been an incredible evening for me and hopefully most in attendance feel the same." Many applauded enthusiastically, but some were not as moved. "I can see there might be some dissension. Depending on how long the questions and answers take we have time for a one or two questions from the audience, please stand if you want to direct a question to our spirit guests."

Rev. Julie King, Head Pastor of Abyssinian Baptist Church, the largest black church in New York and also the largest Baptist Church in the world was selected for the first question. "I am so shocked," she started, "I feel like I was punched in the stomach when Rev. Whitefield said Jesus is not God. If this is true, and truly from Jesus, I feel like I have been lied to all my life, even lied to by God and by Jesus. I don't know what to do with this," Rev. King said wiping a tear from her eye.

"I felt the same way and that's why I argued with Jesus," said Mr. Whitefield, "but Jesus said to me, 'I am still the same Jesus that you told so many people about, my love is the same, my love for you, my love for God, I am still the good shepherd.' Jesus lives in an incredibly beautiful palace in the highest heaven. If he was God, I don't know where he would live. You never 'see' God in the spirit world, as He is only spirit, with no spiritual body like we have. But we can see Jesus."

Rev. King said, "I'm sorry, but I am upset over this. I need to pray deeply about this. Now I need to know what is true."

Jackie responded, "That is the best suggestion for all of us; to pray about all that is being revealed through these messages."

"It is on Earth where all the problems and misunderstandings begin, and then they continue into the spirit world," Martha said. "God chose this time to begin to clear up what the people on Earth believe through allowing the development of the technology to make these visits possible. It has to be cleared up on Earth first. The Earth feeds the spirit world with new spirits, and each one begins exactly where they left off on Earth, believing what they believed during their life and continuing the divisions and mistaken beliefs into the spirit world."

"Before we reach that unity on Earth, there will be a lot of pain and struggle. This will take time, but the process has begun," I said.

Dr. Del Torre said, "We're not going to have time for any more questions and will have to bring this conference to a close. But I think that is a good place to leave it. I am very grateful that the Harvard Divinity School opened its doctoral program for ministry to all religions. I think this is in tune with the messages we have heard from the spirit realms. Amazing. I am so glad that all of honored guests could share this time with us. Thank you and thanks to all who attended."

Reaction

After the Thanksgiving showing of the Harvard Divinity School Symposium the reaction from Evangelical Christian ministers was swift and condemning. Rev. Demston, the Indiana pastor who wanted to create a coalition of Christians to oppose our work, declared that the statement on the Symposium that Jesus was not God that he was a man only, was proof that this intervention from the spirit world was not from God, but rather a clever con job or worse, a demonic deception.

The Southern Baptists invited Rev. Demston and Cardinal Mackay from Los Angeles to join in their opposition to the spirit messages and forming a unified group called themselves, Defenders For Christ. They invited Rev. Julie King to speak at a convention they organized for Atlanta, Georgia to kick off the new year of 2023 defending the trinity. But Rev. King, a Baptist although not a Southern Baptist, declined the invitation. She was still struggling with the Harvard show, feeling there was truth there and certainly was not ready to make any more public statements. Defenders For Christ began running full page ads in the Los Angeles Times, New York Times, Wall Street Journal plus twelve other papers refuting point by point what they objected to in the spirit messages. Their first point was always that this was a hoax and not from the spirit world, or if it proves to be from the next realm to be a product of Satanic forces and not from God.

Another person who was strangely silent was Pope Matthew. Originally he had questioned the veracity of the spirit messages, seeing conflict with Catholic doctrine, but since that initial proclamation he had not added to this statement. We were told that the Pope and his three closest advisors had been receiving some divine visitations. But there was also no censorship of Cardinal Mackay, letting him make his denouncements of this "anti-Catholic propaganda from demonic forces."

In this realm of paradise there are still believers of all the faiths represented, but there is no animosity between the different religions. Only those who loved God and practiced love and service towards others either on Earth or later in the spirit realms as they progressed could even live in this sphere. In the higher realms of heaven there are no separate institutions of religion because people are already filled with God's divine love. Religions are a gift to help us work toward that relationship with God; they are not an end in themselves. As for God, he sees all of us as his sons and daughters; even those in the darkest hell are still his children.

Ali ibn Abi Talib with a full beard and dark piercing eyes, the son-in-law of the Islamic prophet Muhammad and the last prophet of Islam, was asked to lead the council and the discussion on how to approach modern Muslims. We sat on the beautiful rug and were given dates and peach nectar as refreshments by some of the mosque regulars. Ali began with the traditional greeting, "As-salamu alaykum," (peace be upon you). Ibrahem, Muhammad ibn Mūsā al-Khwārizmī, the Persian mathematician, tall with a long face and nose, and Avicenna Ibn Sīnā, the father of early modern medicine shorter, with a kinder face, responded with "Wa alaykumu s-salam wa rahmatullah" (May the peace and mercy of Allah be with you too) and I gave a slight bow of my head as acknowledgement of my respect for their traditions.

Ali said "It grieves me to see the continuing division in Islam, with Muslims killing Muslims. This division began right after the death of the Prophet, though I tried in every way possible to bring unity. It also grieves me to see the killing of innocent people who are non-combatants, through aggressive jihad. This is a perversion of Islam, as jihad is meant to be in defense of the faith, not attacking everyone who is not a Muslim or especially of Muslims killing other Muslims. I saw in a few hundred years after my passing how Islam became the envy of the world in developing science, medicine, mathematics, geography with you two fine gentlemen among many others contributing so much genius."

Avicenna and Muhammad bowed their heads in acknowledgement. "How can we make a plea to the Muslim world for peace and understanding, for acceptance of other views? Our faith demands submission, as that is what Islam means, submission, so it does not leave room for open mindedness. Perhaps a non-Muslim has some ideas. What do you think, Daniel?"

"Ibrahem and I have been working on something for a few months now in preparation for this council. We have three young suicide bombers who are deeply ashamed and repent for what they did, and especially since nothing turned out like they were promised: being sent straight to heaven, surrounded by luxury and virgins. All three died within this last year. One is a Sunni Afghan boy who was sent by the Taliban laden with explosives into a busy marketplace in Kabul. Another is a Shiite boy who was sent by Hezbollah into a Sunni mosque in Lebanon, killing 30. And finally we have a Sunni Iraqi girl of 16 who exploded her backpack full of nails and broken glass at a UN manned checkpoint outside Al Hillah, Iraq, killing soldiers along with many Muslims who were near. We are hoping they will be willing to share their testimonies to help prevent more bombings." I replied.

Ali responded with tears in his eyes, "I am ashamed before Allah, ashamed of all the violence, and now even using girls to kill others. Please, can we meet these three young people?"

"Yes, my wife Martha, is with them now and they are ready to come at any time. We had them sleeping in a healing home until Martha woke them just now. She has been getting to know them," I said.

"We would very much like to meet them," said Avicenna. "Please invite them here" added Ali.

Martha and three young people appeared in the room. The three former suicide bombers were not of this higher level and it could be many, many years before they could begin to heal the pain and suffering their acts had caused to the fatal victims also now in spirit world, to those wounded and to their grieving extended families and friends still on Earth. Martha was shielding them with an envelope of love so they could breathe in this part of heaven. "Gentlemen, it is very good to meet you," Martha began, "I would like to introduce Hussein Zqaq el-Blat from Lebanon, Gahzi walade Muhammad Moqim from Afghanistan, and Nasira Al-Humaid from Iraq."

We all stood up and adding our flow of love and compassion greeted our guests as if they were princes and a princess of heaven. Our respect for them made their faces flush and Nasira began to cry. We could see in their spirits their difficult lives, their horrendous deaths and the hell they were now coming from. Gahzi and Hussein were looking around with their mouths open at this beautiful mosque in the bright sunlight. Hussein said, "The sun! It's so beautiful here! No one's attacking me, no blood, no suffering! Can we stay here? Please!"

Ali reached out and said, "Salam, my children. Be at peace while you are with us. Now you are residents in the spirit world and there are spiritual laws that can't be avoided. You thought you were being righteous and following Allah's commands and that benefits you, but also you went on this mission of destruction for personal gain, to be sent to heaven, to be rewarded, and for the boys to be surrounded by 72 houris to tend to your every need and fulfill you sexually. You found that promise of heaven to not be true and I am so sorry for you. What you have done has caused a lot of suffering and innocent bloody deaths and so much pain. What we sow on Earth will be reaped in the spirit world, even if you were told something else. We are responsible for our actions and the consequence of our actions even if we were told it was a direction from God."[19]

I added, "I'm sorry for you three also and we called you here to see if you would like to help others avoid what you went through. Are any of you aware of the different shows from the spirit world that have been shown on television in these last three years?" Nasira was nodding her head but Gahzi and Hussein had no idea what I was talking about. "I haven't seen any TV shows for a while. Where I lived in Afghanistan was a constant war zone with the Taliban fighting the Americans and the puppet government," Gahzi responded.

"Nasira, what did you see?" I asked. "I saw the show from Indonesia and also the one from Estonia," she responded.

I said, "Good. That's a start. What did you think about the Buddhist Monk, Preecha Willapana, who set himself on fire protesting the Indonesian show and then later from the spirit world when he came on the Estonian show?"

"Well, most of us thought it was a trick by the Americans and that none of the shows were actually from the world of spirit. We know the Americans are experts at special effects, making movies and computer graphics. I wasn't sure, it all seemed very amazing," Nasira said. "But I was being trained to go on my own mission and didn't want to be sidetracked or I would start to have doubts."

We explained to the three young Muslims all about what we have been doing in our outreach to the world. Now, of course knowing what they have been through since coming to the spirit world, they have different views than when they were being indoctrinated for their "martyrdom." We asked them if they would be willing to be on one of our shows, this one directed towards the Muslim world, to explain what happened when they died and where they went. We also wanted to know if they would be willing to have scenes of the hell they were in revealed on the show to help other recruits for suicide missions have a truer vision of what awaits them. We had never shown the true terrible nature of hell in any of the shows, but felt the world now needed to see. It would be shocking to see the bloody and violent hell our young friends were in, maybe too much for many people on Earth, but many were going to similar places if they didn't turn their lives around.

We didn't explain to our young friends that by doing this they would be able to be elevated to a better place by helping many people on Earth make better choices. They had died thinking of going to heaven and we wanted this now to be a choice with no promised rewards and in the end that would benefit them all the more, if they were willing to help others as a true act of selflessness.

Nasira said, "But my family will see me and it will be so painful for them to see me suffering. I don't know if I can bear that. They think I am a hero now."

"Nasira, I feel you have a younger sister, do you want her to follow your path? Can you see that she idolizes you and will do as you did?" Ali asked. "NO! NO, please. Yes, it is better to let people know," Nasira cried out.

"I will help you also," Gahzi said and Hussein agreed with the offer.

"All the people I killed in my mission, they have been attacking me, hating me, killing me over and over even though I can't actually die now. I'm so sorry, so very tired, so afraid to go back to that hell," Gahzi said, visibly shaken.

I said, "That is what sometimes happens in a murder, the murderer and the murdered are bound together in hell, sometimes for centuries hating and attacking each other, until at least one can forgive the other and rise above that horrendous event. It is a compounded tragedy where the victim also goes to the same hell bound by the fixation for revenge. Do you know that around Hitler in hell there are hundreds of otherwise innocent Jews who were killed by his decrees, hating him, clawing at him, throwing things at him, tearing his hair and bloodying him even to this day?[20] I have seen this. It is beyond horrible. There are also many Jews who rose above the cause of their death, their families and communities destruction and are now doing well, freed from the hate and from the passion for revenge."

"Gahzi you come from a people who do not easily forgive and who never forget. By killing them they are bound to you until you can pay for what you have done to them, as if that is even possible, or you will need some strong intervention; prayer, forgiveness and love from those affected on Earth."

Martha added, "This is why it is so important that we reach out to the Muslim world, to end this cycle of murder and revenge. And this is why we need you three to share your stories to help your fellow Muslims on Earth."

During our planning for the Muslim outreach we had a conference with Edwin, Jackie and Mike. They knew they were not the right people to address Islam but would pool their resources to see if they could find the right people. On addressing their staff and friends they found that Enrique and Barbara Rodriquez, the Christian couple who had been at the Thanksgiving potluck three years ago, were involved in an inter-religious group, Peace Through Religion. One participant was a Muslim woman from Pakistan whose husband was a broadcaster at Al Jazeera America.

Enrique and Barbara had never joined the staff at New Shambles but they were fascinated by the work and had seen all the shows. They agreed to be the facilitators for a meeting with New Shambles and Taahir and Pakeeza Leghari. Pakeeza turned out to be a strong advocate for peaceful Islam and was outspoken against jihadist terrorism. Her husband, often in front of the camera, was more diplomatic and careful.

The Legharis were astounded at the request to reach out to the Muslim world from the spirit world but once they met Gahzi, Nasira and Hussein through our interface at New Shambles they began to get excited. A week later Taahir brought the Vice President of broadcasting, Ken Johnson, from Al Jazeera America to New Shambles to meet the three young Muslims, along with meeting Ali ibn Abi Talib, Muhammad ibn Mūsā al-Khwārizmī, Avicenna Ibn Sīnā and Ibrahem. Martha and I also sat in as representatives of Jiva Satata and Edwin, Jackie and Mike were in the background at New Shambles. From the spirit world side we were once again in the main hall at the mosque Ibrahem represented.

We decided that it would be filmed privately with no prior publicity as a safety precaution and in fact the whole project would be a close kept secret until it was released. Mr. Johnson would look into a broadcast first from Al Jazeera in Qatar in Arabic and later from Al Jazeera America in English so it wouldn't be attributed to an American production.

During this time, as we waited for the show for the Muslim world, Ali took the three young Muslims under his care. They were extremely anxious that they would be sent back to hell, and their repentance grew all the stronger as they saw the consequences of their actions.

Chapter 18
Progress Report

Outreach Efforts

Garuda and Rajinda called for a comprehensive report on progress on several fronts, the Catholic approach, the Buddhist outreach, the beginning of the Muslim outreach, the website, the opposition in general, and the response in North Korea, China, India, the United States and Russia were of particular interest. It was a much smaller meeting than the previous one with only Martha and me, Father Sean McCoy, Jerry and Qieci. We were invited to the higher celestial realm, to Garuda and Rajinda's home for this briefing. They covered their home with a protective spiritual shield so we could be comfortable in the more rarefied atmosphere.

Jerry was reporting on the website and the visits to the site from everywhere in the world, including from some of the few privileged people in North Korea who had access to the world Internet and not just the countries' internal intranet, when we all had an overwhelming sense of peace and love flood us. We had a visitation from Jesus and Buddha. Jesus, especially was a brilliant light that filled us with the presence of God's love in every cell in our body. Buddha, who had not developed or taught a personal relationship with God, was a lesser but still brilliant light. He only experienced God's love much later in the spirit world and that was through Jesus reaching out to him. Jesus was extremely grateful for all the work we were doing and wanted to share God's pleasure with us. Buddha shared how he was leading many of his followers in spirit world to reach out to Buddhist on Earth through dreams and pushing them to see our shows and the website.

After our unexpected holy guests departed it took us a while to get back to our reports. Jerry was especially moved, this being his first encounter with divine spirits and he was not able to finish his report. Qieci took on the next briefing on his work in China and North Korea. North Korea was becoming a nation divided with more and more people having dreams and even daytime visions and the government was becoming desperate in their suppression. Sixteen people had been executed and hundreds had been sent to labor camps after they publicly proclaimed the existence of God and an afterlife. Now many citizens were no longer afraid of repercussions with the threat of death, imprisonment or even harm to their families and having hope for the first time.

China was a much less closed society but the problem for the governing body of a growing belief in eternal life was no less frustrating. Even prominent members of the Communist party were openly talking about the love of God and the need to end the government oppression of religions and the crackdown on unauthorized home churches.

Qieci reported that he was developing a personal relationship with the Dalai Lama through the Buddhist leader's old Dell computer. It was modern enough for the Internet to work as the Dalai Lama kept track of news reports online and would Skype with his followers regularly. Qieci, sometimes along with the Buddha, had weekly calls and the Dalai Lama was very interested in the spirit world. In fact he would also tweet to his online flock and open the transmission to Qieci and Buddha to anyone who wanted to watch the conversations. Though the Dalai Lama only represented one small part of the Buddhist religion he was generally respected by the Buddhist community worldwide. Many leaders and followers of different sects were connected to him through his tweets and would eagerly watch these incredible interchanges with the spirit world.

This represented a shift in our outreach with Buddha actually appearing to people on Earth. I thought it interesting that Buddha had not told us personally of his appearing to people on Earth through the Dalai Lama's transmissions, perhaps not wanting to testify and uplift himself. Though we had that breakthrough with Buddha showing himself to people on Earth, Jiva Satata was not ready for Jesus or Mohammad to make an appearance.

The Dalai Lama was far more receptive to change than the Pope and the Catholic hierarchy. Sean McCoy reported that the Pope and many Cardinals had dreams and daytime visions of Mother Mary, along with many saints and though they knew the messengers and the messages were true they were very reluctant to make public proclamations. The Catholic populations on the other hand were much more open to the possibility of heaven reaching out to Earth, where mysticism and spiritual miracles have long been their lifeblood. Many priests and some Bishops were encouraging their parishioners to see the spirit shows and to go to RebirthinSpirit.org to learn about heaven and eternal life.

Next Martha and I split our reports with Martha sharing about progress in Russia and the former Soviet Union countries along with India and the United States and I reported on our progress in preparing for the

Muslim show.

"Our shows in Hungary and Estonia had an enormous impact on Russia and most of the countries in the former Soviet empire," Martha began. "I think that the 70 years of forced atheism on the area only created a greater desire to know about God and to seek spiritual truths. The people are hungry for connection and we think this area of the world is ready for individual transmissions from spirit world."

"We are feeling that also," said Rajinda, "but we want it to be a unified opening throughout the world. There are many beautiful people martyred from former communists' countries who are eager to help their relatives and countrymen and women. Since we haven't opened the computer connections to individuals yet the spirits from this part of the world are descending on mass through dreams and inspirations."

"Thank you, Rajinda," Martha continued, "Now, I'm sorry to say with one of our first shows being in India, India is a mixed bag. We are seeing a rise in Hindu fanaticism and some riots in Mumbai and New Delhi denouncing our spirit message. India has always been one of the most devout countries in the world and yet this new view on truth we are offering doesn't give Hinduism much to stand on, with their belief in millions of gods and also in reincarnation. They do still respect Buddha as one of their avatars, so perhaps through him we can reach more people. The politicians and the media are for the most part more secular than the general population and are afraid to endorse anything that challenges Hindu belief."

Garuda said, "We knew that India would be challenging and that's why we had our show there. It's difficult because there is not one person responsible for starting this religion and Hinduism can be traced back thousands of years before Buddhism or any other religion. Did you know there are millions of Hindus in spirit world who are still waiting to be reincarnated, some waiting for hundreds or thousands of years? So it is not just a problem on Earth but also in spirit world. With strongly held beliefs for those who pass into spirit world we have to be very careful with who will be allowed to use our technology so as to not add to the confusion. There are thousands or even millions of Hindu spirits who would mistakenly assure their descendants that they will reincarnate soon. So we still have a lot of work to do in India."

Rajinda asked, "How about the United States?"

Martha responded, "The United States has many groups who are opposed to our shows and message, the strongest being The Defenders of Christ. There is less of a unified support, which emphasizes some of the challenges for America. Individuality is so sacred in the United States that everyone has his or her own opinion and perspective. Worldwide we see about 20% acceptance of the spirit world we have revealed. For the United States it is closer to 17% although the largest number of people who visit our website from any country are from America."

Rajinda said, "Don't be discouraged, considering we have been active in our outreach for less than three years, 20% acceptance worldwide is outstanding. How many thousands upon thousands of years has the Earth been feeding spirit world and filling hell with uninformed or misinformed people who had no idea of the value of their lives or what to expect at their passing. 20% of 7.5 billion people is 1.5 billion people. More than a billion people are now looking at their own lives, looking at their belief in God, looking at their relationships and whether they have been a more positive or negative influence on others. How many of these people would have lived selfish or destructive lives and now have a chance to change the direction of their lives and to come to a wonderful place in spirit world. This is just the beginning and it will get even better."

With tears in her eyes she pushed back her beautiful blond hair, Martha said, "Thank you Rajinda, for putting it in that light. Yes, it is wonderful and we are so grateful to be helping so many people."

"Thank you, Martha, Jerry and Qieci. We still have some major initiatives in plan. Daniel, I believe you are going to report on the progress of the Muslim show. Why don't you share how that is going now," said Garuda. "Please invite Ibrahem and Ali to join us for this part of the report, thank you."

Report on the Progress of the Muslim Show

I sent out a thought invitation to Ibrahem and Ali ibn Abi Talib and they appeared in the room with us.

"We have filmed much of it already, so let me show you what we have so far, and then you can make any suggestions. Our plan is to show it the day before the Islamic holiday of Ramadan begins in 2023. Ramadan is celebrated during the ninth month of the year based on the lunar calendar. It is one of the five pillars of Islam and is celebrated by fasting from sunrise to sunset for the 29 days of the month. Because it is a holy time families are much more connected during Ramadan. With the fasting everyone anticipates the evening so they can have a meal together. We hope many of their discussions in those evenings to be centered on our show and about spirit world. Next year Ramadan will begin on Thursday, March 23 and our show will be presented on Al Jazeera in Qatar on March 22nd and a week later from Al Jazeera America," I explained.

By thought power I created a screen resembling what people on Earth would see and started the program and a message appeared on the screen in Arabic and English, "The following program was created in the spirit world, the place all people go after they pass from their earthly lives. It is a message of hope and peace for all Muslims." At first the screen shows the outside of the golden mosque and then the view flows into the meeting hall and then focuses on Ibrahem sitting on a comfortable chair. Ibrahem began, "As salamu alaikum wa rahmatullah wa barakatuhu, greetings to my Muslim brothers and sisters, my name is Ibrahem Al-Omari. I lived from 1810 to 1883 in what is now Iraq but was then part of the Ottoman Empire. Although I lived to a good age of 73, I died of the Bubonic Plague when it swept through my village. Muhammad, may peace and blessings of Allah be upon him, has given us the commandment to create this show to reach his loyal followers on Earth. We will have several guests on this show, some lived hundreds of years ago and three have recently come into the spirit lands. This show will have some very graphic scenes, so please consider not allowing children to watch this."

Ibrahem continued, "Our first guest is Ali ibn Abi Talib, who is the cousin of the Holy Prophet and was the first young male to accept Islam at the age of 12. Ali's father was Abu Talib and both Muhammad and Ali grew up in his home. Ali is respected by all sects of Islam and so we wanted to have him as our first and honored guest for this show."

Ali ibn Abi Talib walked in wearing clothes from the era in which he lived. He sat at the table and slightly bowing his head, said, "Assalamu Alaikum" to Ibrahem and to the audience through the camera.

Ali told how it was growing up in the home of the prophet and what it had been like when he came to spirit world. He implored all Muslims to respect all other Muslims and to end the division and bloodshed. He quoted the Quran that Christian and Jews are our brothers under Abraham.

Ali then introduced Muhammad ibn Mūsā al-Khwārizmī and Avicenna Ibn Sīnā as scientists and mathematicians coming from the golden age of Islam from the 8th century until the 14th century. "Did you know Muslims used to be the envy of Europeans of whom many would come to our Universities to further their studies of the sciences?" Ali began. "Avicenna Ibn Sīnā wrote over 450 papers on philosophy, medicine, astronomy, alchemy, geography and geology, psychology, Islamic theology, logic, mathematics, physics and even poetry. He wrote the Book of Healing and the Canon of Medicine which became standard medical text in universities throughout Europe and the Middle East for over 600 years."

"Muhammad ibn Mūsā al-Khwārizmī was a famous 8th century Persian mathematician, astronomer and geographer known throughout Europe and the Middle East. Muslims on Earth today did you know of these men and many more who helped to advance science and knowledge? Did you know the world is indebted to brilliant Muslims like these fine gentlemen? What has happened to Islam in these last hundred years?"

"Now we attack schools, killing children and teachers. How have we come so low, so bestial? Why have we disgraced Allah with this sacrilege? Muslims should strive to be the leaders of research and education, starting with educating young boys and girls throughout the Muslim world," said Avicenna. "Anyone who teaches otherwise is an apostate, a false teacher and should be reeducated to stop teaching hateful messages."

"It is a crime that many Islamic schools and certainly most madrasas only allow one book, the Quran. You should have books on philosophy, mathematics, astronomy, history, psychology, biology, and so much more, plus all other sacred books of the other religions," Muhammad added. "Educators should be raising up a new generation of enlightened leaders, not bringing up the children only to be used as suicide weapons spreading more pain and suffering. Islam is meant to be a religion of peace and compassion. Allah is being misrepresented as a murderous God who delights in the massacre of innocents. We have made God small minded and impotent, relying on suicide bombers to bring victories. You must know God sees all people as His children and loves every person intimately, passionately."

Ibrahem then invited the three young people into the hall. "The next part of this show will be hard to watch for many people but this is the most important part of our presentation. We have three young people who recently came to the spirit lands, but did not go to heaven as they were promised. Instead all three went to a very terrible hell of their own making. All three were suicide bombers, but from different nations and representing both Sunni and Shi'a Islam. Hussein Zqaq el-Blat, a Shiite, was sent by Hezbollah into a Sunni mosque in Lebanon, killing 30 other Muslims. Gahzi walade Muhammad Moqim is a Sunni Afghan boy, who the Taliban sent into a busy marketplace in Kabul to kill and maim as many as possible. And finally Nasira Al-Humaid, a 16 year old Iraqi Sunni girl, exploded her backpack full of nails and broken glass outside Al Hillah in Iraq at a U.N. checkpoint killing soldiers and many Muslims."

Hussein and Muhammad each shared their horrific stories, how they were raised with the need for revenge as their daily food, going on their missions of death, and finally the dark, bloody, violent hell they were in before being brought into a higher spirit world and asked to share their stories for this show. While they were speaking there were videos showing the actual deep, dark and violent hell they had come from, terrible and disturbing. Those who had been killed by Hussein and Muhammad were shown beating and clawing at these two young terrified men in the two separate videos. Ali said, "As you can see, although promised paradise, instead Muhammad and Hussein were blown into hell along with those victims of their missions who now hated them, despising them for ending their lives. Without rest they were attacked over and over for the few months since their bombings."

Nasira, a pretty girl wearing the traditional black hijab, then shared her story, "I was born in a Sunni family in Iraq in the time of the shift of power from the Sunni minority to the Shiite majority rule. As a hated minority that had once ruled with fearful powers under Saddam Hussein there were a lot of attacks on people in my neighborhood. When I was seven, my father was caught one day returning home from his work in construction, two days after he went missing his body was dumped on the street, bruised and bloodied. My older brother went to find who had done this and was also tortured and killed."

She continued, "I was devastated and angry. With my hate and anger I joined other women who had lost their husbands, fathers, sons or brothers. For the men who die as a martyr in jihad, they are promised 72 houris (full breasted, wide eyed virgins) and 80,000 servants, for women they are promised their husband or one man for eternity. I had no chance for a husband, but one good man for eternity was better than my life on Earth. But mostly I was angry and wanted revenge. I went to one cleric and said I wanted training to become a martyr. He set me up with a group of women who were also interested in holy revenge. I was trained and educated for a year before it was determined I was ready and a target was chosen. My mother was very upset with my choice for martyrdom, feeling she already lost too much. She cried and tried to stop me from attending this training, even threatening to turn me into the authorities. So two weeks before my mission I left my home, left my mother without saying good-bye."

Tears were in Nashira's eyes as she continued with her story, "I learned how to make a backpack bomb full of broken glass and nails. I wasn't told where my mission was until the day of the event and while on the way from Bagdad to Al Hillah. There was a young man also in the van and we were told that he would first approach the checkpoint manned by Iraqi Shiite Military and U.N. soldiers. The other bomber would set off his bomb, then after ten minutes I would approach the crowd gathered after the blast, walk into the middle of them and set my bomb off. Our bombs had two ways of detonation, by a button we could push or if we got scared our handlers would detonate it remotely by cell phone."

"It didn't work out as smoothly as they'd said it would. The boy was so nervous and sweating and they had to push him out of the van. He sort of stumbled toward the checkpoint and he looked so suspicious the soldiers told him to stop with guns aimed at him. There were people near him so the guys in the van detonated his bomb. People were running all around screaming, and police and an ambulance came into the mess. Then I left the van and walked over to the crowd and near the checkpoint and pushed my button," Nashira continued.

Ibrahem leaned over and put a hand on Nashira's shoulder "Are you alright? Take your time."

Nashira took a deep sigh, wiped her eyes, and sat for a moment. Then she continued, "All the promises of paradise were a lie. Between the boy and my bombing we must have killed about 34 people because they were all there, thrust into spirit world the same time we were. They were stunned and disoriented at first as we were also. But soon they realized what had happened and saw me and the boy. Some had lost arms or legs or were shredded to a bloody pulp by the shrapnel in our bombs. But bloody and grotesque they came after us. There were a few who accepted their deaths as Allah's will and didn't hate us. I saw bright spirits come and take them away, including a the few children killed, I guess to a higher plane. I never saw them again. It was a very dark and terrifying hell we were in. I had no concept of time or how long I was there. I was always running, trying to hide. They would rip my flesh, tear my eyes out, hold me down and beat me or rape me again and again with so much hatred burning in their eyes. Then I saw it wasn't just those who had died by our bombs but there were hundreds or thousands of people here attacking each other, ripping and tearing and killing over and over, but you can't die, so you recover and are attacked again and again. I could never imagine such a hell was possible."

"Nashira, why are you willing to share your story?" asked Ibrahem softly with deep compassion in his eyes.

"I expect to go back to that hell after this time of sharing my story and I am terrified. I just hope that I can help to stop this insanity, that some people will listen and stop training people for suicide missions, that young people will hear this and choose a different path for their lives, instead of hate and revenge, they can choose a life of forgiveness and love. Please people, don't do what I did, I beg of you, please don't," Nashira said weeping.

Then a magnificent light came down and surrounded Hussein, Muhammad and Nashira. It was so bright with no obvious source, it was swirling and embracing. The three were crying with their faces turned upward in this heavenly tempest.

Ali ibn Abi Talib stood and looked at the camera and said, "God has blessed these three young people who did a terrible thing, but now by sharing their stories with millions watching this show they have been forgiven and will remain in this realm. They came here with no promise of forgiveness or that they would be freed from hell. This was a completely unselfish act for all three and God is now surrounding them with love. But there are thousands of suicide bombers and their victims who are not as fortunate and are still in the hell they created, or for the victims who are bound to their murderers through their hatred and resentment, they are also stuck in hell until they can forgive and seek for God. There are laws in the universe, if you create pain and suffering for others, you are responsible even if you were told it was for God or Allah. You don't go to paradise by killing and maiming others no matter who told you otherwise. We are all God's children, no matter the religion, race, or nationality. If you want to live with God then love His children, serve and forgive everyone. Stop the suicide missions, stop the killings, stop the hatred!"

Back in Garuda and Rajinda's home, with that the video ended we all sat in silence for a time. Finally Sean McCoy responded, "Ali and Ibrahem, that was very well done, very powerful. What do you think the response will be in the Islamic world?"

Ali said, "For the peace loving Muslims they will applaud this and will use it as a way to help end the violence and the suicide missions, but for those who thrive on the sectarian conflict or on hatred of others they will denounce and will perpetrate even more violence. Anything we do in addressing the violence will cause more violence initially, but we believe the good will triumph in the end. We, of course, not only believe this but are mobilizing the Islamic spiritual world who desire peace, to influence their descendants and fellow Muslims on Earth."

Chapter 19
Outreach to Islam

The Show, the Aftermath, and Another Show

On the day before Ramadan began on Wednesday, March 22, 2023 a show ran on Al Jazeera in Qatar called, "The Way of Peace is the Way of Love," a quote from the Prophet Muhammad. For protection of the station and those involved in the production, there was no advanced promotion of the show. A week after showing in Qatar it was shown on Al Jazeera America, deciding that it was better to have a little time between the shows. The shows were added to RebirthinSpirit.org and soon were being copied throughout the internet.

Although no one on Earth was given credit for the broadcast someone hacked into All Jazeera's computer system and found that the Vice President of broadcasting, Ken Johnson, had promoted the show to management and was responsible for both broadcasts in Qatar and America. On Friday, April 8, while leaving the studio in Washington D.C. a man on a motorcycle drove up to him and shot him three times. He died on the steps before the paramedics could arrive. A group calling itself, Americans for Islamic Caliphate, claimed responsibility, saying Al Jazeera had promoted a lie about Islam that could not be tolerated.

A young man from Somalia, Abu Ubeid Omar, uploaded a video on an Islamic chat site saying he had been preparing for a suicide mission, but the night before his mission he had a dream and Hussein Zqaq el-Blat, one of the suicide bombers from the show came to him and begged him not to do this and showed the hell he had experienced. He knew it was more than a dream and made a plea to all Muslims to not go on anymore suicide missions. The plea was shown on Al Jazeera with Abu's face blurred. Abu went into hiding, but not being very sophisticated he was discovered at his aunt's house. The house was burned to the ground, killing Abu, his aunt and three of his cousins.

Since the show, suicide bombings were down dramatically throughout the world as recruiters were finding it harder to find young Muslims who didn't know about the show with the three young suicide bombers on it from the spirit world.

Ibrahem initiated a new show with the original three bombers along with Ken Johnson and Abu Ubeid Omar. In my view, this show was a three punch knock-out. When Ken was on the show he named his assassinators along with all who had taken part in the planning. He gave their addresses and aliases they used. They were soon found and arrested. He promised that from the spirit world they could see all who were working in the shadows and will expose them. This posed a problem for the legal world, as nothing from the spirit world could be admitted into evidence. But the fugitives could be caught with the assistance from the spirit world and then evidence collected later.

Mr. Johnson's statement sent shivers through the world, not just for Islamic extremists, but people everywhere. Suddenly there were talk shows, newspapers, magazines with questions about all sins, big and small, being seen and exposed by spirits. This made a lot of people nervous, anxious of their own discretions.

The second shocker of the show was Ali ibn Abi Talib who came at the end of the show and again introduced himself as the Prophet Muhammad's cousin who grew up in the same home as the Prophet. As he was speaking he began to weep asking what has become of Islam, saying it has become a murderous religion, losing sight of truth and goodness. He said Muhammad was so ashamed of Muslims today. Ali asked how Muslim could be attacking other religions when the Prophet told them not to do this, but rather to protect them. He then read a letter from the Prophet Muhammad:

"This is a message from Muhammad ibn Abdullah, as a covenant to those who adopt Christianity, near and far, we are with them. Verily I, the servants, the helpers, and my followers defend them, because Christians are my citizens; and by God! I hold out against anything that displeases them. No compulsion is to be on them. Neither are their judges to be removed from their jobs nor their monks from their monasteries. No one is to destroy a house of their religion, to damage it, or to carry anything from it to the Muslims' houses. Should anyone take any of these, he would spoil God's covenant and disobey His Prophet. Verily, they are my allies and have my secure charter against all that they hate. No one is to force them to travel or to oblige them to fight. The Muslims are to fight for them. If a female Christian is married to a Muslim, it is not to take place without her approval. She is not to be prevented from visiting her church to pray. Their churches are declared to be protected.

They are neither to be prevented from repairing them nor the sacredness of their covenants. No one of the nation is to disobey the covenant till the Last Day."[21]

The show ended with the final punch with Ali asking Muslims to find the heart of God in service to others, including other religions. He said that the Quran forbids idolatry and yet they have idolized the Prophet, treating him like God. Muhammad should be shown the same respect as God's many prophets, including Jesus and Abraham, but not idolized. No one should be killed for questioning Islam, the Prophet or the Muslim world, but rather should be shown the love and service of true Muslims. And finally he stated that being a Muslim is not the final goal, but just a step towards finding God, just as being a devout Jew, Christian, Bahá'í or any other seeker. All are good and honorable, but all are just stepping stones to finding a relationship with God. He stated that in the higher heavens there are no Muslims, Christians, Jews or any religions or denominations, only sons and daughters of God, full of light and love and to reach that level was our true goal as humans.

Chapter 20
Samuel Wakes Up

Samuel Begins to Respond

While we had been in Garuda and Rajinda's home planning the Muslim shows I felt for the first time that our son, Samuel wanted to see me. We were not free to leave our work until after the shows and then Martha who had felt it also said we need to go see him. Jerry was busy with Patrick working on the website so Martha and I went together. We sent a thought to Samuel that we were coming and appeared near his cave.

The two guards were outside and for the first time we looked at them and let them feel our compassion also. The larger of the two jerked his head back and bared his teeth and the other man was visibly shaken by our interest. "He is waiting for you, go inside," growled the second man averting his eyes.

Samuel was slumped on a rock and glanced up as we entered. I let him initiate the conversation. "Father, I don't know how to relate to you. I have always hated you even though I never knew you. You weren't there when Mom was treated like a leper and lost everything. I hated everyone and I hated my life." He paused and looked at me for the first time.

"Sam, I'm so sorry, I have always been there for you and Mom. I have always loved you but you were closed to me," I began slowly.

"Mom has told me about the better places in the spirit world and though I've been in this hell for I don't know how long, she said I could still change my life. What year is it on Earth, anyway?" Sam asked. "Its 2023," Martha said. "Damn, that's over 200 years," Sam said. "I had no idea."

"Sam, we could bring you to our home for a short visit. What do you think?" Martha asked.

"I don't know. I guess so. How do you do that?" Sam stammered

"We'll show you," I said and we came and over to hug him covering him with a spiritual envelope. When we stepped back we were in our living room. Samuel gasped and fell back hiding his eyes. "Oh my God! Oh my God! The light! The air!"

After giving him a moment to adjust we helped him up, trembling with bulging eyes. Speechless we helped him out our front door to the garden under the warm, beautiful sun. Sam fell to his knees on the grass weeping, "What a bastard I've been! I never knew! What a shit I've made of my life. I'm a monster. How can you love me?" Sam wailed. Even with our spiritual protection he was finding it hard to breathe and after a few more minutes we returned to his cave.

Chapter 21
Spirit Centers

Outreach on a Personal Level

Garuda and Rajinda sent a request for Joseph Fourier, the French scientist who was the first to speak to Edwin in our beginning outreach, Martha and me to meet at Nexus Magna, our new hall for communication with the world. When we were in the elegant conference room Garuda and Rajinda walked in with another couple and introduced them as Victor and Helena Sobolev who had lived in the Russian city of Mytishchi, which is northeast of Russia's capital Moscow, on the Yauza River. They experienced the Communist takeover of Russia and the expansion of the Soviet Republic into the USSR. They came to the spirit world 50 and 54 years ago respectively. Officially they had embraced Marxism and became card carrying members of the communist party; though in their homes they secretly maintained their belief in Jesus having come from the Orthodox Church before the revolution.

Before the meeting officially began Rajinda came over and held Martha and my hands saying, "We are watching you reach out to your son, Samuel. We are helping you and you may have felt that." "Thank you," we both said together.

Rajinda then looked around with a smile on her lovely face and love shining from her eyes and began the conference, "We are ready to begin the outreach on a personal level, allowing some people to connect with their ancestors or relatives. We will keep it very much controlled so old and misleading concepts are not continued by less advanced spirits or by anyone from any level, for that matter. Many people on Earth are likely to believe anything that comes through our channels so we have to be very careful with our connections. As we discussed earlier we would like to begin in countries from the former Soviet Union. There is the ironic benefit of atheistic communism working to eradicate all churches and all religions, in that we now have a more open platform to teach about God and heaven without as many preconceptions. Victor and Helena will spearhead our outreach into Russia and former countries under the Soviet Union from the spirit world side. We have worked with them before on other projects but this is their first introduction to the work of Jiva Satata."

Garuda, with his deep brown eyes, smiled also and said, "When we first made our outreach to Earth we connected to Edwin Jackson and his group of friends. One of his friends, Ben Stine and his son, Patrick, coming from a Russian Jewish background, still have family ties to Russia and have been there recently. We spoke to them about setting up a center in St. Petersburg under the New Shambles name as a place where people could come to seek a visit with someone in the spirit world. They are working on getting the license and all the legal steps to make that happen.

Also from our show in Estonia, the lady host for the show, Elif Vaher, was very moved by the whole experience and has asked to work with New Shambles. She and her husband are also willing to set up a center for connecting with spirits. Mr. Stine will also oversee the center in Estonia, since he has been with New Shambles from the beginning. We had a video conference with Victor and Helena Sobolev from the spirit side and the Stines and Vahers on Earth and we see this as a strong team of dedicated and enthusiastic leaders. As more people in the future accept our approach we might move away from specific centers and just let people use their computers in their homes or even through their cell phones, but for now we need strict diligence in maintaining a pure message."

Garuda continued, "Joseph how big is your technical group and how many connections can we maintain at the same time? Could we have, say, a thousand conversations simultaneously when we are ready?"

Joseph responded, "Well, why don't we start with less than a hundred, even maybe just twenty or so and work up to larger numbers as we become more experienced. We will need a large group of people who can find the person in whatever level they are in the spirit world, meet with that individual first and see if they are a good candidate to communicate with someone on Earth. I think we can't make promises to anyone on Earth that they will be able to meet whoever they want. We certainly don't want to bring someone from the lower spirit levels, not without serious supervision."

Garuda looked at Martha and me pleasantly and said, "Don't worry about who will find the spirits, Joseph. We have that covered. We would like Daniel and Martha to lead the group of volunteers to do the search and vetting of spirits to determine who is ready for communication to Earth. We have over 3,000 people from this level of spirit world who have shown interest in this project. Within a few days we would like you, Daniel and Martha, to meet with this group and begin training them. As we advance we expect a much larger group of volunteers to come forth. What do you think of this?"

"We are here for the long run and are thrilled to now take this to another level," I said with a grin. "What will be our goal in this training?"

Rajinda responded, "First of all, make sure everyone is sharing the same understanding of God, as a loving parent who created this universe as a gift and to be a joy to his children. We don't want any dogma or traditions from any religion, church, sect or belief to muddy this clear understanding of God. God is the source of all love and all life. God is the unified perfection of male and female so you can relate to God as your father or your mother, whatever fulfills you most at the moment. Second, God condemns no one, we create our own environment while on Earth or at least we create our response to our environment and later we create our own version of heaven or hell in the spirit world based on how we lived our lives, how we treat others, and whether or not we let God's love flow through us on Earth. God doesn't punish but He will always challenge us to grow and be open. Third, the best way to serve God is to serve other people, not with expectations of a reward, but because we are all one family under God."

Garuda added, "We selected the 3,000 because they share these views of God, so we want you to train these first volunteers to become trainers for others. When a person first comes to one of our centers on Earth seeking to communicate with a spirit they will have to give us information on the person and a photo, if possible, and then return in a few days, we can decide how many days we need, to be told whether or not we can bring that spirit to a meeting.'

"We have told New Shambles to not charge anything for the original meeting, and to set up a standard price chart if a meeting can be arranged or messages sent. If a meeting is not possible information about where the spirit is in spirit world can be shared and messages can be given between the spirit and the people on Earth. They know that this is a service, not for them to grow rich with, but they do need to charge a fair price to keep the centers active and for the workers to make a reasonable living. We know there will be a lot of fraudulent spirit centers popping up that could easily take advantage of people and become rich.

That is one of the side jobs of your volunteers to keep these charlatans from taking advantage of people," Garuda said with a chuckle.

"That is why we want New Shambles, which is already famous throughout the world for the shows and website, to create authentic centers and to charge reasonable fees. Their name and reputation are their greatest assets. We expect once these centers start their service they will quickly become known throughout the world and many countries and communities will also want a New Shambles center. Edwin is very aware of this and has been training many people to be able to lead future centers. I know they advertised in the United States for expatriates of nations throughout the world who might want to return to their countries and set up New Shambles centers. The response has been quite encouraging."

New Shambles Spirit Centers

The Stines set up a New Shambles Spirit Center with the name in English and Russian, Novyy Shambles Dukh Tsentr, near the Neva River in St. Petersburg, Russia on Liteyniy Prospekt. The grand opening, set for November 1, 2023, was advertised through newspaper, radio and local television stations, including RTR SPb TV a national station that broadcasts throughout Russia. The Spirit Center was near a large residential and business area and close to a home of a cousin of Ben Stine. The center was large enough to have ten smaller rooms with computers and video cameras and seating for five people in each room and a conference room for larger groups. Along with the communication rooms, there was a central reception area, a secure room for the server computers, and a large office pool area with separate offices for management.

Ben's cousin from his mother's side, Vladimir Maklakov, was hired as the operating manager, leaving Ben to oversee this center, the one in Estonia and future centers as they grew. The center in Estonia was scheduled to open in February of 2024.

After the center in St. Petersburg had been open for a few months Martha and I sat in on several communications to see how they were conducted and what we could do to improve the service. Here are some we overheard:

On the computer screen the people on Earth could see the Spirit Facilitator and interacted with him, a pleasant looking Russian man.

Earth side facilitator: "We have here Sabrina who requested to visit her father, Ivan, last week. She has returned to see if that is possible."

Spirit facilitator: "I'm very sorry, but Ivan is in a lower spirit level, but he has asked Sabrina if she could pray for him. Honestly he is ashamed at how he looks now and could not bear for Sabrina to see him."

Sabrina: "I know that my father did some terrible things, including to me. I'll pray for him and want him to know that I am trying to forgive him."

SF: "We can open verbal communication with Ivan, but not visual, would you like to talk to him, Sabrina?"

Sabrina: "I'm a little afraid. I guess I will try for a short time."

SF: "Ivan what would you like to say to your daughter?"

In a clear audio voice the Earthly participants could hear, "Sabrina, oh my God! I'm so sorry. I didn't know, I didn't believe in heaven and hell, God, all that. But what I did to you, to your mom, I was a terrible man. Still I knew it was wrong, but didn't care," weeping, gasping, Ivan continued, "You said you would pray for me. Oh thank you. It is more than I deserve."

Sabrina: "Dad!" Sabrina crying, "I...I hated you for years. But now, I can't carry that anymore. You would get drunk, and... Why? I will pray for you every day because I don't want you to be stuck. They told me at the center here, that you can grow in spirit and slowly go to higher spheres. I want you to become a good man, a good father, like you were some times. It is so hard."

Ivan: "Oh thank you Sabrina, you have given me some hope. It is so dark here, so cold, so many terrible people. Thank you for praying." The transmission ended with a great wail.

SF: "That is all for now, but I think you can help him grow, Sabrina. Your love for him can be a guide to him and he will feel your love directly. You don't know how much that will comfort him. Pray that he can see and feel all the pain he caused to you and your Mom, that he can then repent of the suffering he has caused. Then he can begin to take responsibility and to open a tender heart."

Sabrina crying said: "Oh my God! That cry at the end, how horrible. Thank you for making this possible. This has changed my life, showing our lives are eternal. That was my father! He is in so much pain, you could hear it!"

We hadn't discussed just having verbal conversations when the spirit was in a low spirit world and were impressed with the Russian spirit who improvised and made this encounter so very powerful. It would be terrifying for most people to see the deformed hideous shapes of so many people in hell, especially if they knew the person from Earth.

The next communications was a happier experience. Maria had lost her daughter, Tiffany, who died at age seven, three years ago from encephalitis. Maria brought in her husband, Tiffany's dad and Tiffany's two brothers and one younger sister. They used the conference room for this larger group.

Earth side facilitator: "What a nice family, we have Tiffany waiting in the spirit world. Is everyone ready?"

Maria: "Oh my God! Is it possible, please bring her on!"

The screen flashed and then a pretty young girl with bouncy blond hair was on the screen. Everyone in the room screamed and yelled. "Tiffany!" they all shouted together.

Tiffany: "Oh hello, Mom, Dad, Jacob, Samuel, Terri! It is so good to see everyone. Isn't this amazing? Oh, I love you all so much."

Maria: "Oh, my baby! Look how you have grown. You would be ten years old now."

Tiffany: "I am ten, Mom, nothing has changed. I live in a most beautiful place, with other children who died young. We all attend school here together, not like school on Earth, but we are learning so many amazing things. The people, who are taking care of us here, love children and are so encouraging. I feel your love for me all the time. I am so lucky to have such a loving family. Not all the kids here come from such good families."

Dad: "Tiffany, when you passed away, were you in pain? Did you suffer much?"

Tiffany: "No, I just remember fading away, losing consciousness, and the next thing I know I woke up here. They had me rest in a healing home for a few weeks before my life really started here. Right now I am in a hall they set up in spirit world for communicating with people on Earth, but they said, if we want I can show you my home and meet some of my friends here. A camera person will go with me. Her camera has a screen on it so I will still see you, along with anyone we meet. Would you like that?"

Her sister, Terri: "Oh my God, I very much want to see your home and meet your friends!"

Dad: "Please do Tiffany. This is all so new to us, so amazing."

Tiffany looked back and said something to the lady filming and instantly they were in a beautiful field with flowers all around. There were many children running and laughing and also several dogs, cats and even a llama. A warm friendly looking woman with an engaging smile came over and greeted Tiffany. She put one arm around Tiffany's shoulder and said, "Hello Tiffany's family. We are so happy to have Tiffany with us here. She is very bright and helps us with the younger children."

Tiffany: "Mom, Dad, this is Aunt Olesya. She has been taking care of children here for over 400 years. Can you imagine that? She is teaching me how to make flowers, real flowers that are alive."

Olesya: "Let's show them our homes, and where we teach our classes."

They walked up a path next to a lush lawn and as they did several girls ran over and joined them, hugging Tiffany and one held her hand and walked with them."

Tiffany: "Family, this is my best friend here. Nona, this is my family. I love them."

Nona with short brown hair said with a cute smile: "Hi, everyone. Tiffany has told me a lot about you."

A small brown terrier came over and barked and spun around. Nona said, "This is Scampers. He was my dog from Earth. He died before me and was here when I came over."

Dad: "We saw that on New Shambles, with their dog, Shambles. That is so wonderful."

Olesya: "Here is Tiffany, Nona, and two other girls' cottage. Each cottage has an adult who lives with them. For children who come here before their parents they join us here or go to one the thousands of other places like this covering all the different cultures and languages on Earth."

The cottage looked to be made of stone, with a chimney and windows with curtains covered with flowers. The door was an arched dark wood with a little window decorated with hummingbirds and flowers made with colored glass. Roses of many colors were all around the small porch.

Tiffany: "I made all these flowers. Isn't that neat?" As Tiffany began walking over to the flowers, the blooms turned toward her and vibrated, Tiffany picked one white rose, and said, "Mom, this is for you. I will put it in my room and it will stay fresh as long as I love it! I wish you could smell it, it is so refreshing!"

Maria, with tears flowing freely: "You made the flowers, how is that possible? Thank you for the rose! Wow, I am so happy. I could not imagine any of this. I'm so happy for you, Tiffany. Death is such a harsh word, but now it lost all its power over me. I was so devastated when you died, so sad for months. Now I am overjoyed! Such a weight has been lifted off my shoulders. We couldn't wait to use this service once it became available. I'm so glad we did."

The family was led through the children's' rooms by the lady filming the interaction, and although it isn't necessary to sleep, each child had a bed if they wanted to take a nap, a closet and a chest of drawers. There was a common room that was full of art from the kids. They were brought to a larger building that had many classrooms, although they were told that a lot of the lessons were out in the field of study.

The children ranged from infant for those who died at birth or were still born to eighteen with appropriate care and instruction for each age and level. Their classes included astronomy, healing arts, plant and flower creation, architecture, languages, literature, art, music, singing, history of many cultures and so much more. These may sound boring, but here in the spirit world they are very exciting. For the study of astronomy they actually could visit other planets, go inside the sun if they wanted without feeling the heat, go to and see other galaxies, stars, planets up close all travel through the power of thought. For history, they would often be visited by the actual people who were central to the history and these guests shared what their lives were like, and could give them video-like glimpses of some especially important events. They could meet people of any age, any culture and learn from them. If they studied the history of art or music they could meet many of the masters in person. It was such an uplifting experience for Tiffany's family that we were filled with so much hope for our work through this interchange.

The third interaction we witnessed was between a husband who lost his wife to cancer. Once the Earth side and Spirit side facilitators were ready they let the two have their privacy.

Konstantin: "Galina, wow this is incredible. How are you? What is your life like there?"

Galina: "It has been unbelievable. I feel so comfortable here. Everyone is so friendly and there is so much to do all the time. I'm sorry I left you alone and abandoned you. Are you OK?"

Konstantin: "I'm doing well, considering. It's good you went before me, because I don't think I would be in heaven. They would have to drag through hell to find me, and I don't know if they do that."

Galina: "Now Konstantin, that is just not true. You are a good man. I hope you are looking for a new wife like we talked about."

Konstantin: "Well, now that I can see you again, I find this very difficult. There is a lady that I have become close to, but I feel like I am cheating on you now that it is obvious you are still alive."

Galina: "You are only 45 years old and you need love in your life. Our kids need a mom also, one who is alive on Earth, who can hug them and guide them. Please, if this is the right woman and if you love her, you are free to marry her. You have my blessing and more than that, my encouragement to pursue this relationship. How is she with our kids? Does she have her own children?"

We could see that this was a mature conversation requiring sacrifice from both parties. We also knew it would not always be so fruitful with those passing on complicating relationships on each side of life.

We met with Ben and Patrick Stine and the center manager, Vladimir Maklakov through their large screen, along with the leaders assigned to this center from the spirit world in the center's conference room. I smiled at everyone and said, "Hello, everyone. Those conversations were amazing to watch. This is so powerful, so emotional for everyone involved. The doorway to the spirit world has been truly opened to the world!"

I continued, "You've been open for over three months and we would like to know how it has been going, what the response has been like, what you've learned, and what we can do to improve the service. Hi, Patrick, it's good to see you continuing to do such great work. You really helped us breakthrough in the beginning." Martha smiled also and waved at everyone. We felt a lot of love for and from this dedicated group of people. Patrick waved back, grinned and said, "I have an announcement to share and also an idea to run by you when it is my turn."

Martha winked at Patrick and said, "Why don't you go first then, Patrick."

Patrick replied, "First I'll give my suggestion, since my announcement might take all the oxygen out of the room." We all chuckled and looked intrigued. "I would like to set up a website, linked to RebirthInSpirit.org of course, as an outreach to youth throughout the world to teach about the value of life on the Earth and how that affects our eternal life, including some of the videos made of young people in the spirit world. We want the message to be that it is cool to be good; cool to be loving and unselfish to attract the youth. It could include some good hearted rap and songs that will appeal to the young, bands from on Earth and some from the spirit world."

"Excellent idea! We do need to reach people younger before they go in the wrong direction. Who would you work with?" Martha asked.

"The original group of kids that were at Edwin's house when this all started along with Jerry in spirit world and whomever he wants to add. And that brings me to my announcement; one of those original kids was Elsa, my girlfriend. Remember that it was Elsa's dog, Shambles that became our name. Well..."

"Yes, go on," Martha said with eyebrows raised.

"Well, we are engaged to be married!" Patrick said.

"Yay! That's wonderful." Pausing as a thought came to her said, "Hey, would you and Elsa like to be our youth outreach ministers or maybe there is a title with less church related sound, since we don't want to alienate any religion?" Martha asked. "How about we call it Youth Outreach Ambassadors?"

"We actually talked about doing just that and would be excited with this challenge. I'm the computer guy and Elsa now has a degree in early child development from Stanford University, so that is perfect. Here is another idea. Our marriage is set for Thanksgiving of this year in honor of that first meeting from spirit world. My Dad and I will be flying back to the States for the wedding. We would like to have the wedding at New Shambles headquarters in Oakland and we want all our spirit friends to be there also," Patrick proclaimed with a big smile.

"Oh! This is very good news! We are so happy for you! We'll be so honored to attend using your large screen at your headquarters. We can have a celebration here along with yours. We'll let our celebration planner, Anselma Glaus, know. You haven't met her yet so we will introduce you so you can coordinate the planning. A new historical moment, our first marriage to be celebrated on Earth and in the Spirit lands at the same time. How exciting!" I said.

"When we are married Elsa will join me in our work in Russia, so she is trying to learn some Russian," Patrick added laughing, "And that's not an easy language to learn."

Martha said, "Well since all the oxygen is gone, let's all take a break and then we can continue in fifteen minutes."

"Ben, please give your report on your work in Russia so far, when we return, and then maybe Vladimir could go next," I said.

When everyone was back Ben shared about setting up the center in St. Petersburg and how the response was escalating quickly. They already had a backlog of interested parties and would be hiring more people to keep up. We promised them whatever needed support from the spirit side and would speed up the process of finding the spirit wherever they were in spirit world and vetting what type of communication would be allowed based on whether the spirit was in a good level or not. Ben talked about working with Elif Vaher and her husband, Juhan, in Estonia and the great response there. Since Elif was a well-known television personality she worked a deal with the Estonian station, Eesti Televisioon, to create a new show on the spirit world, using some footage from the interactions at The New Shambles Spirit Center, with permission from all sides, including those in spirit world. With this added exposure the Estonian Spirit Center was also growing quicker than they could keep up.

Vladimir shared about the personal work with the families looking for a relative. He said they have also received requests from business associates seeking advice from a former partner or CEO and also interest from law enforcement to help find the truth in current and unsolved cases. So far they have not pursued anything beyond family or ancestral relations. He sought our advice on what to do about these other requests. Also some families have sought out a parent who passed on without leaving a will and they wanted to know how the deceased wanted his assets divided.

"We will leave this to your judgement on a case by case decision," I said. "If by meeting a business associate this will bring a peaceful resolution or solution, than we see no reason why not to let them pursue this. But we might suggest a higher price strategy for non-family meetings. As far as clarifying a person's will, that can get very sticky, possibly escalating a fight between survivors. You might be safer to let the courts decide this, but again we will let you use your own discretion. But please have your lawyers write up some forms that anyone using the service will not hold you responsible for whatever response from the person in spirit world."

I continued, "We knew this exposure would also be an issue for resolving legal and criminal cases. As an example, if a murdered victim could identify who actually murdered him or her from the spirit world that could clear things up quicker than having to build a case against someone. At this point I think we should hold off on expanding our service to allow police or lawyers use of the spirit centers. Let's keep this focused on family meetings for now."

Ben said, "I agree completely. Oh and we met with lawyers before we even opened up and all participants have to sign a very clear form that clears us of any responsibility from where the person ended up in spirit world or what might transpire in our meeting. We make this very clear from the beginning of each negotiation that they will likely be in for many surprises when they contact someone who has passed over. If they have any reservation we suggest they return when they are ready to receive whatever comes. There have been so many people who were sure their loved one was "saved", only to find otherwise. They want to blame someone and we refuse to be drawn into their misconceptions. We also felt it necessary to hire a security firm that has an officer here every day we are open in case someone reacts with aggression. But most meetings are rewarding for both sides, thank God, like the ones you witnessed earlier today."

To close the meeting we had a prayer together. It didn't matter that the Stines were Jewish and we were from a Christian background, since we all believed in the same loving God.

"Thank you for all your amazing work. We love you all. I wish I could give you all a big hug," Martha said.

"And thank you for all your support. This is an incredible time we live in," Ben replied.

New Shambles Spirit Centers Expand Worldwide

After the successes in Russia and Estonia there was growing requests to open more Spirit Centers from almost every country. The first one to open in the United States was in Hayward, California run by the growing staff at the headquarters in Oakland. Edwin had trained over 70 new managers who were ready to return to their home countries to open up new Spirit Centers. Part of their training included a trip to Estonia and St. Petersburg to see a center in action.

The first wave of new centers included South Africa, Korea, Israel, Mexico, Canada, Panama, Brazil, Germany, Italy, England and Turkey, the first country with a Muslim majority population. Each new center would have three managers trained at New Shambles International, Inc. along with 100 spirits who we had trained from the original 3,000 that Garuda had assigned to us. They would then hire the remaining staff from the local populations from each country.

With the expansion of the spirit centers the opposition also grew and was becoming more unified. Defenders of Christ tried to shut down the headquarters in Oakland with protests and even legal action claiming New Shambles was defrauding gullible hurting people who might believe anything about a loved one who had passed on. From the beginning New Shambles was not set up as a non-profit to avoid any dispute on whether the fee for contacting people in spirit world should be taxed or not. So included in each price sheet was the state taxes. They were a legal corporation that paid taxes and reported all income. The court found no basis for the lawsuit and it was dismissed.

Mike Templeton and Jackie Nagorski, along with Tammy McNeal who now had her own corporation whose show was syndicated on 40 stations in 23 countries, were still having television shows throughout the world. They tried to have a show in each country that was to host a Spirit Center and would promote the grand opening for each center.

In Hamburg, Germany there was a credible threat from a domestic terrorist group against opening the Spirit Center. They decided to open anyway and on the opening day a bomb was thrown through the front plane glass window and one of the trained managers, Helga Guttenberg, was killed. A left wing non-Communist group, "Radikale Gegen die Religion" claimed responsibility. Her picture was shown on news shows worldwide and on New Shambles next show in Italy, Helga came on. We had a strategy that could not be countered, if anyone was killed promoting the open viewing of the spirit world they would be the next guest on one of our shows. People had a hard time disputing that someone who was on international news who was killed in action was now addressing the world audience from the spirit world.

Turkey was another place where security was critical and the Prime Minister dedicated some national armed forces to patrol outside the center. After President Recep Tayyip Erdoğan's attempt at a third term was declared unconstitutional in 2021 the country had to work hard to become a secular nation once again, refuting Erdoğan's push toward an Islamic centered government. The popularity among Muslims visiting the Spirit Center showed there was great hope for further inroads into Islamic Countries. We felt the two Muslim shows we sponsored were pivotal towards a greater acceptance of an inclusive spirit world. Extremist Islamic groups were looking for a new strategy as the recruitment of young suicide bombers was no longer fruitful. From our side there was a push from high level Muslims to visit Muslims on Earth through their dreams and thoughts to encourage peace and honor for all religions, for all people.

To our overwhelming surprise we received a request from the Secretariat in the Vatican, Cardinal Kamukama originally from Uganda, who asked about the possibility of setting up a Spirit Center in the Vatican. The Spirit Center in Rome, Italy was busy all the time and it was rumored that some of the people who visited the center were from the Vatican.

The Italian center was headed up by a former priest, Nicolo De Luca, who had been living in the United States and answered Edwin's ad looking for center leaders. Mr. De Luca was now married and with his American wife, Linda, they had a secret meeting in the Vatican with Cardinal Kamukama. They were told that Pope Matthew was very interested in the work of New Shambles and of Jiva Satata, but he would not make any public endorsements at this time. As soon as they met Cardinal Kamukama they recognized him as someone who had arranged to meet his parents from the spirit world. It had been a very heartwarming meeting of parents and son with many tears.

The De Lucas, with permission from New Shambles headquarters, were very supportive of another center in the Vatican but had some stipulations; it would be run like any other center by someone trained in New Shambles headquarters, not every request for a meeting would be granted but would be scrutinized like any other request, depending on where the person was in spirit world and what frame of mind they were in and all meetings would be recorded and become part of New Shambles archives. All the archives were secret and confidential and would only become part of a show on television or online if all parties agreed in writing, including those in spirit world. The fees would be the same as in other spirit centers. The Vatican agreed with all these conditions but also wanted to retain their own records for the Vatican archives of any meeting. We were fine with them keeping a copy of all meetings.

The Spirit Center of the Vatican was set up in secret led by Nicolo and Linda De Luca and another couple took charge of the Rome Center. Before any requests from the Vatican for any meetings was entertained, there was a request from Jiva Satata. The three Popes who had requested to work with Jiva Satata wanted to have a meeting with Pope Matthew and his close advisors. Pope Matthew was very enthusiastic for this meeting with the three popes, St. Gregory I (Gregorius), Pius IX (Giovanni Maria Mastai-Ferretti) and Pope John Paul II (Karol Józef Wojtyla) along with Father Sean McCoy. Pope Matthew requested that Martha and I join the meeting, since he had apparently seen most of our shows and so had some familiarity with us.

World News

There are spirits who have the responsibility to keep track of all the major news happening on Earth. For the overwhelming majority of people in the spirit world they are not so connected with what transpires on their home planet, as they are too involved in their own pursuits in the spirit world. Those who are recent arrivals are likely to reconnect when someone they know will be passing over, but for those who have been in the spirit lands for hundreds or thousands of years they have little connection with Earth. One exception is for those who are involved in welcoming and guiding new spirits to their new land and their new home, as Martha and I do. In order to effectively relate to the newcomers we have to have at least a general idea of what modern society is like.

Another exception is the department of spirits who actively monitor major events on Earth giving regular reports to the higher realms, especially those who are involved in guiding humanity on the path God has set for the restoration of his family. This department was known as Terra Firma Activities and Rajinda had set up a division to monitor all events related to the work of Jiva Satata and New Shambles, who was responding positively or negatively on a large scale, how different organizations and different religions were reacting to the latest revelations.

We were now within our fourth year of outreach and the major staff in Jiva Satata decided on getting a full update from Terra Firma Jiva Satata on our effect on Earth. On February 2, 2024, Earth date, Joseph Fourier, Anselma Glaus, Father Sean McCoy, Qieci, Pope John Paul II (representing the three Popes in spirit world involved), Jerry Tanner, Ibrahem Al-Omari, Martha and I met at Terra Firma Activities and were joyfully welcomed. Garuda and Rajinda did not attend this meeting, leaving it in our hands and we would report to them later.

The center was beautiful and impressive with huge glass windows overseeing a rushing stream that was forming rainbow explosions of color and soft harmonious sounds that gave us a feeling of tranquil peace. There were thousands of spirits involved in watching events throughout the world, events of successful efforts towards reconciling conflicts between nations or events that would lead to greater conflicts. These reports would lead to spirits activated as needed to hot spots in the world.

Spirits involved in helping the earth by helping individuals overcome prejudices, misunderstandings, anger, resentment or temptations would be sent to people they might have a connection with. Whenever emotions are at a high level this becomes a magnet for spirits of a lower level to intervene for selfish purposes, to draw negative energy to feed on. To balance this, spirits from higher realms would also arrive to help bring a more peaceful cooperative spirit to the interchange.

People living on Earth have no idea that there are spirits around every person all the time. Some are good spirits working as spirit guides while others are there with selfish or even evil intent. Each person also has a "guardian angel" though they are spirits who were once humans on Earth. Angels are spiritual beings who never had a physical body and that God created in the beginning to assist in the creation of the universe and later as helpers and messengers for His children, men and women. So just as every person has at least one "guardian spirit," every person also has two angels attending through their lives.[24] The guardian spirit, a more apt name, is someone who has voluntarily been with a person from birth until death. There are other spirits who come and go as needed. Most people have at least a dozen spirits around them at any given time, many have more than forty spirits and some influential people might have hundreds of spirits around them all the time.[25] Every high energy activity draws even more spirits, both low spirits and higher spirits. Mob mentality can only be understood when you also consider the heightened spiritual magnetism of highly charged emotional crowds.

Terra Firma Activities was not only observing or even reacting to events but also promoting thoughts and activities that will help humankind create a more beautiful, peaceful and loving world. Where there were thousands of spirits who work at the center there were billions involved in influencing people on Earth. Many thoughts that come into a person's mind are actually from spirits that are nearby, whether they are temptations to engage in hurtful activities from a lower spirit or to do good selfless acts that will benefit others inspired by thoughts from a higher spirit close by. Besides the spirits that might be sent to someone, people attract spirits that are similar to themselves, evil people attracting evil spirits, good prayerful people attracting spirits who also love God, and so on. There is always a struggle going on for each person, for their thoughts, their actions and ultimately for their souls. Though we have also seen that people can repent and change, even in the spirit world.

We were brought to the Jiva Satata division and met with a gracious and vivacious host. Graciela was a high energy spirit, originally from Chile, and a friend of Rajinda. We were brought into a large room where hundreds of spirits were watching views of activities on Earth, not through an electronic screen but by connecting spiritually through the people involved. In this room were people originally from all over the world, from all religions and nationalities. They were watching areas and people they had a connection with, people of the same religion, same culture, or similar background.

Graciela told us, "Rajinda said you would be coming here and want to see the reaction, the response to your efforts to open the spirit world to Earth. Is there a specific group that you want to focus on?"

I said, "First give us a general response from the major religions, with some samples we can watch thrown in. We want positive and negative examples. If there have been significant events anywhere we would like to know those, and see what happened. We would also like reports on progress in China, North Korea, the United States, India, Russia and Eastern European countries, South America, and African nations."

"OK, that is close to what we expected," Graciela responded. "Well, since you had two shows aimed at the Muslim world, let me start there. Some countries are trying to suppress your website and all shows your groups have been behind. These include some predominately Shiite or Sunni nations: Iran, Saudi Arabia, Somalia, and Yemen. All groups considered to be terrorist groups are very upset that their sources for suicide bombers have been drastically diminished through the testimony from your suicide bombers. Five Fatwahs have been declared to strike your spirit centers, attack your personnel and anyone involved in your shows. But your people on Earth are very brave and continue at the risk of their lives."

She continued, "There are some Islamic nations, mostly those who have a good relationship with the United States or European countries that are actively supporting the message. These include Jordan, Turkey, Arab Emeritus, and Dubai. Other countries are very wary of supporting or attacking your efforts, including Pakistan, Afghanistan, Iraq, Egypt and Indonesia. Among Muslims worldwide you are gaining some ground, with close to 20% believing that the shows were actually from the spirit world and that Islam should be a religion of peace, respecting other beliefs and promoting knowledge and goodwill."

Ibrahem said, "That is great news! We can defeat those who promote hate and destruction by sharing the truth. And as we did before, if someone is murdered by some fanatic then they will be on our next show from spirit world."

We heard other news, some good, some challenging, all essentially hopeful though.

In North Korea 430 people were executed for spreading the news about a living God, another 1,350 were sent to hard labor camps including whole families. Those 430 Koreans are now being received in heaven and from what we were told were eager to continue the work of spreading the news to those left behind in the People's Republic of Korea.

China was also cracking down on the message by trying to suppress all internet access to RebirthinSpirit.org and other sites that were exploding with shared videos from spirit communication. It was looking like a losing battle for the government.

Estonia was on fire. With the well-loved couple Juhan and Elif Vaher promoting the Spirit Center on their own show and with daily examples of people meeting their loved ones in the spirit world they now expanded to four more centers in Estonia, each with a waiting list. The St. Petersburg center is less than a five hour drive from the Tallinn, Estonia center so there was a lot of coordination and shared activities. Together these two main centers are creating plans to open Spirit Centers in Latvia, Lithuania and Belarus along with more centers in Russia.

Spirit Bound founded by Rev. Osamu Shigiyama in Japan was now an international movement welcoming people of all religions who want to practice selfless service to God by helping less fortunate people. Many of those associated with Spirit Bound were also welcomed volunteers at Spirit Centers.

Defenders For Christ in the United States continued to grow attracting Christians from many denominations who refuse to believe the message that Jesus is not God, hell is not eternal and that people of other faiths are also in heaven. They unsuccessfully launched legal attacks to stop more Spirit Centers from opening in Kentucky, Louisiana and Texas. Lawyers for New Shambles defeated these attempts with first amendment arguments for free speech. Rev. Demston was becoming well known for his speaking tours, especially in the South where his message was more accepted. Cardinal Mackay was less visible in his opposition after finally receiving a warning from the Vatican.

Rev. Julie King, who had spoken up at the Harvard Divinity meeting was now a regular visitor to the Washington D.C. Spirit Center. Her mother, who had been a famous pastor, had passed into the spirit world eighteen years earlier and confirmed to her daughter that Jesus was a man, a man who had reached divinity but was not God, and she had met him many times. She said this was a hopeful message because Jesus is the example; anyone can be like Jesus and achieve divinity or oneness with God. If Jesus is God then he is unreachable, placed on a pedestal only to be worshiped, not emulated. Her Mom's love for God and Jesus were exemplary in the Baptist Churches. The two powerful women cried their joy at being able to see each other again at the Spirit Center. Rev. King was leading her own church to this new understanding of Jesus and they were taking it all in and supporting her because of their love for their pastor. Rev. King was invited to speak at several television talk shows and showed video excerpts from her meetings with her mother at the Spirit Center.

The United States was not leading the way in the transformation but the belief was growing, especially as more Spirit Centers open. There were pockets and clusters of more enlightened people in different parts of the country. In the California bay area, where New Shambles began there was a growing movement on the Universities and Colleges. Berkeley University requested their own Spirit Center and the Dean of Religious Studies, Dr. Sarah Wyman, was becoming a strong advocate.

We were told that Berkeley had been the lead on campus protests in the last century, with students clashing with police and the government protesting war and other causes. The message of peace might have been distorted during those times of upheaval but we felt it was perhaps appropriate that this University might lead the nation in a new movement to be one family of peace. Other schools across the country were opening the discussion about the spirit world surprisingly with new curriculum classes being added to address these questions. The argument was this was not of a particular religion which would be frowned on at a public school, but whether Christian, Jewish, Muslim or Buddhist there was electricity in the air about living all together and respecting each other. So it was more a social, moral issue that could be addressed in a public or state run institution.

Africa, at least the predominately Christian nations, had always been more open to spiritual influences than most of the world, but not always towards good spirit world. With a growing exposure to spirit world it was becoming clear that whatever we do to others in a hurtful way will become a spiritual debt that must be paid. The positive belief in helping others was growing, replacing the negative use of spiritual influences such as; voodoo, the local witches, the animist worldview or the practice of placing hexes on enemies. So far our influence had not helped bring respect or unity in thought between the Muslim majority nations and the Christian majority, Roman Catholic or Protestant.

In the Republic of Congo a village witch was beaten by a crowd and chased out of town. In response New Shambles then posted a video on RebirthinSpirit.org appealing to villagers to not spread violence as a re-action to misunderstanding of spiritual forces explaining that until the present day the whole world was ignorant of spirit laws and realities. Our message was never that "we are right, and you are wrong," but rather together we can build a beautiful world if we love and honor our neigh-bor, find the spark of God in each person, forgive others, forgive your-self, be patient, and most important, to seek a personal relationship with God as our loving parent.

One continent that was experiencing a rebirth was South America in-cluding Central America and Mexico. This area of the world has always been heavily religious and spiritual, often mixing Catholicism with in-digenous beliefs and practices. There were several shows and webpages dedicated to showing excerpts from videos made at the spirit centers and more pastors and priests were getting involved, transforming the Christian message.

These were just some of the reports we heard and we were inspired. The impact was incredible and would only grow. There would be no re-turning to the time of ignorance and division. Whether countries, reli-gions or groups were accepting the new version of spirit world or not, they were having to deal with this challenge. Of course we still have many years of work to go, but we were ready. Correcting misconceptions on Earth was only the beginning. Each person has to develop their own relationship with God, and knowledge of afterlife in the spirit world was only a starting point in the process of becoming a good loving person. We didn't want to eliminate religions as they were organized ways that people could work together to improve lives. We only wanted to shine a light to help them find their way.

We were also seeing the impact on the spirit world, as far more people who were passing on were more aware of what was happening and going to better places, to higher levels than they would have if they had continued in their small minded lives. That was always the overall goal, to help people live fruitful, meaningful lives full of love and goodness and then with that foundation later enter the spirit world on a higher level. The highway to hell now had some detours. We knew that after tackling the misconceptions on the Earth, fixing the enormously vast spirit world would be a much bigger task.

Chapter 24

Inter-Realm
Conference

World Conferences for Scientists, Engineers, Inventors, Physicians

Joseph Fourier, the French scientist, approached Garuda and Rajinda with a request. "I have been talking with some of the scientists and we would like to initiate some conferences for scientists, engineers and inventors on the Earth together with scientists in our realms. Is this the right time to share our knowledge, our discoveries, and the possible uses on Earth? In each field of science we have made incredible progress and yet it has only been revealed so slowly before."

Garuda replied, "We have also been thinking along these lines but we would also like to see other conferences including some to help the medical establishments improve their knowledge, along with mental health experts. These sciences are only half-sciences since they were unaware of the spiritual world and the affect spirits have on everyday life for people on Earth. We want to do this on a world level so participants could come from all over the world or connect through the internet from anywhere. But I want to caution you also on what inventions you share with people. Please clear that with us and we will check with higher authorities as usual with any invention or new understanding in physics or other sciences. Remember the world is not a peaceful place yet and many new direction for science or new ideas for devices that could be weaponized will be turned into weapons by someone."

Joseph said, "Thanks for the reminder and we'll be very careful and clear everything first. Before I approached you we investigated the possibilities and think that we should have these conferences through the United Nations headquartered in New York in the United States."

"An excellent idea and hopefully Edwin and New Shambles will be able to secure a conference hall at the United Nations. Suggest that to them and let them see if it can be done. Also please work with New Shambles and Daniel and Martha to find the best people, both on Earth and the spirit world, to work with in each field to make these conferences work. We not only need great scientists, engineers, and physicians but also the best people at organizing, marketing and administration on a world level," Garuda replied.

Joseph replied with a chuckle, "Alright, I should have figured it would be a lot bigger than what I was thinking. I know some excellent doctors and medical scientists and a few other people. Let me talk with the Everhearts to get this process going and they can work with the New Shambles side."

Then Rajinda said, "And Joseph, when you do have your first conference, be sure to tell Edwin to invite Richard Fish, the Leader of the American Atheists, and any of the scientists who are with his organization. He is an astrophysical scientist and though he is unaware, many of his ideas were sent to him from Einstein and some other scientists here."

When Joseph told us the plan for the conferences I saw another aspect of the medical side that had not been mentioned. Martha and I had been involved in some healing circles while on Earth as we saw how prayer and directed thoughts could help people gain power over their infirmities. For the medical conferences we wanted to include people who had been healers while on Earth along with some healers currently on Earth.

Modern medical research had veered away from spiritual assistance with the rise of the scientific method. Before institutionalized medicine, prayer had always been an integral part of any work in the healing arts. With a push from spirit world, more recently there has been objective and scientific research into the benefits of prayer and positive thinking to assist in healing, and this was a step forward. Some research was also proving that when a person had a belief in their own healing, they healed faster. Eventually the physical world would understand the power of thought in their realm also.

Science and religion were proving to be estranged brothers that were now finding the value of each other again. With the opening of the gates of knowledge from the Spirit side and now with the Earth working together mankind could advance very quickly in science, engineering, healing, mental health and really every other field of research.

We contacted Edwin of New Shambles who saw the immediate value of these conferences but also felt this would stretch New Shambles into fields they were not ready for. He called a meeting of his staff to see what could be done to accommodate this new branch of outreach. Stan and Irene Peterson suggested that they could open a new corporation under the New Shambles, Inc. umbrella that works with the United Nations to sponsor these conferences. Irene was already the Human Resources

Director for New Shambles and Stan had been working under Jill Tanner as a videographer, along with creating documentaries with HBO on the spirit world phenomenon that was shaking the Earth. New Shambles had a working relationship with HBO ever since producing the Harvard Divinity School show together.

The new branch corporation was called Shambles World Conferences, Inc. with Stan Peterson as the CEO. Irene Peterson remained with New Shambles but gave her staff the job of advertising and hiring for the new corporation. By July, 2024 the new corporation was viable and began promoting the desire for conferences through RebirthinSpirit.org. The idea of inter-realm conferences electrified the scientific, engineering and medical communities.

Retail, Pharmaceutical, Chemical, Medical, Communication and Engineering giants in the world also took notice and wanted to help fund the conferences, with the hint of the possibility of the unlimited new technology and inventions that could be translated into products developed and sold. Stan held them at arm's length until the conferences became a reality and they could see what would come out of them. But he also let them know that he was keeping them in mind.

To Stan the conflicts become obvious and complicated. Who owns the rights to new inventions and new technology that come out of interaction with the spirit world? Stan worked with Edwin to strengthen both organizations' legal departments and also hired a top New York law firm to represent them on corporate and property law. If he did accept funding from any of these corporations, he wanted a clear legal contract that would allow any new scientific paths opened to be available to everyone, not just those businesses providing funding.

Shambles World Conferences, Inc. reached out to the United Nations and then were directed to connect with UNESCO. The United Nations Organization for Education, Science and Culture, or more commonly called UNESCO, was founded in 1945 with its headquarters in Paris, France. UNESCO was immediately interested in hosting conferences that would enable scientists on Earth to work with scientists from all ages past in the spirit world. To us, this was the highest level acknowledgement that our work was receiving some world level acceptance.

The first conference was announced on RebirthinSpirit.org for October 21st to 26th starting with an introductory conference on the first day and then breaking into three separate groups focusing on Science and Engineering, Medical Advancement, and The Physics of Our Universe. All of these initial conferences would be more general, as each of the three separate conferences could be subdivided into a large number of disciplines. From this initial conference in October the different branches of science, engineering and medicine could plan future conferences.

HBO would be filming the conferences that would be held in the UNESCO headquarters in Paris. The news of the conference being held in his native country of France, instead of New York, made Joseph Fourier very happy.

The First Inter-Realm Conference of Science

October 21, 2024 The First Inter-Realm Conference of Science began with an opening talk by Rajinda projected on giant screens in the egg shaped hall where the plenary sessions of the General Conference of UNESCO are held.

Rajinda was dressed in a beautiful flowing robe that seemed to be alive with images of waterfalls, trees, birds and other animals all moving as if it were a film projected directly onto her dress. She began with a bow of her head in respect and a dazzling smile. "Friends on the Earth and friends in the spirit world, welcome to The First Inter-Realm Conference of Science. I want you to know that God is very pleased with this meeting. For many centuries science and religion or another way to say it is, reason and faith, have been antagonist to each other. But do you realize that this division in the search for truth was God's desire?"

She continued, "If those who sought scientific explanations for biology, astronomy, chemistry, physics, mathematics, engineering and all other fields were hampered by religions the world would have remained ignorant of all the things God wanted you to explore and discover. Not to put down religions, but God wanted you to be free to transcend limiting beliefs so you could objectively discover the secrets of the universe that God created so you could advance to this modern world. I say modern world and yet you have just begun to realize your potential knowledge. The rise of humanism, secularism and even atheism was not evil but rather was God's desire. Can you believe that?"

"Before the advent of science, anything that could not be explained was attributed to God, angels or miracles. The world needed people who would not accept that explanation, but would dig deep to find how things work, how to use the laws of the natural world to create the advanced world you now enjoy. We can look at Galileo as an example of a scientist hampered by religion, at that time, the Roman Catholic Church. For those who need empirical proof, who test and re-test all hypotheses, until a theorem can be called reliable and used to advance knowledge and apply that knowledge in practical ways to help the whole of mankind, we applaud you. Is this how you thought this conference would start?" There was a loud burst of laughter, applause and exclamations.

"Many of you here have never believed in God, the spirit world, eternal life, angels or in any spiritual phenomenon or religion because there was no empirical proof," Rajinda added. "I now understand some of the atheists here have attended New Shambles Spirit Centers in various countries and connected with loved ones who have passed into the next stage of human existence. Have you now received the empirical proof that there is more to your existence than your time on Earth? In this conference you will meet some of the giants in your fields that you admired, who though died years or hundreds of years ago are still involved in the pursuit of knowledge from the spirit world. They are eager to share with you and together help mankind advance faster than was ever possible before. Is that exciting?!" There was a roar of approval and anticipation.

Rajinda continued, "You will find that many modern inventions were received in dreams. You may not have realized it, but that was intervention from the scientists in the spirit world helping you in your discoveries. Let's look at some examples: Albert Einstein creates theory of relativity from a dream he received as a teenager, Niels Boher realized the structure of the atom while sleeping, Friedrich August Kekule von Stradonit said the discovery of benzene which revolutionized the production of cars, rubber, fuel, clothing, plastics, and explosives came from a dream, Dr. James Watson realized the shape of DNA while taking a rest, and Larry Page came up with the concept for Google using searchable databases to website links from a dream. Many of you here may be able to relate to this form of inspiration."[26]

"But please promise me that the knowledge you gain together will be used for the betterment of mankind, not for more horrible weapons or any destructive purposes. Raise your hands to show me that you agree with this and promise." It looked like everyone raised their hand, some raised both hands and some stood up and raised their hands.

"Before I pass this on to the MC and to the conference staff I want to give you a hint. Explore the power of thought. Everything in the spirit world is the product of thought, the homes, buildings, transportation, communication, the clothes we wear… by the way, how do you like my dress?" There were some shouts of approval. "This dress, the fabric, the moving scenes are all a product of my thought and of my heart. All here is created by thought but it is not like magic that you want a house and think it into existence. Rather it has to be planned out, how many rooms, the size of each room and it may take three or four or a large group as we saw with the raising of Nexus Magna shown our site. This takes people working together, each an expert on different important parts of the construction but working together with concentrated thought before the house comes into existence. And it is a substantial house, just as substantial as a house in the physical world."[27]

Rajinda continued, "Think of this, the universe was made for you, for all mankind, and yet to get to the nearest star traveling at the speed of light would take over four years and the trip might not even be worth it." Several people laughed. "You know that so far you can't travel anywhere even close to a hundredth of the speed of light. What about the systems that are millions or billions of light years away? Forget about them, right? Is there anything faster than the speed of light? What about the speed of thought?"

"This power of thought will be unlocked when you realize that when God created you, me, everyone, He did not create you as a separate being, rather you are an extension of God, there is no separation. God is alive in you, in your neighbor, in all things. God's heart is in you, not a copy, not separate heart, God's own heart is in you.[28] You will be able to do amazing things, miracles, impossible things, when you realize God within."

"God bless you all, God bless your families and God bless your research and discoveries." Many in the audience had a stunned look on their face as they realized what Rajinda was implying, then there was

a high spirit level, but also not hell; a grayer area than where we lived. The people seemed happy, clustering in groups with various musical instruments, singing and performing together. Because we were focusing on finding one person, Mr. Harrison, we were drawn to a group outside a small house with a simple garden and we recognized our man as the one singing and playing a sitar, an instrument that apparently originated in India.

We sat and listened for a while. The music was slower, more mournful or perhaps more thoughtful, than what we had seen in the videos. A young-looking woman approached us and asked us if we had been Beatles fans. No, we replied, we lived a few hundred years before but were interested in speaking with George when there was a break. "I'll introduce you to him, and by the way, my name is Tanya," Tanya said. Tanya had shorter black hair with cute dimples on each cheek and her blue eyes were shiny and bright. We introduced ourselves and could see she admired or even really loved George. We guessed that she had been what she identified as a "fan" of at least one of the Beatles.

When he was done with the song he was singing, Tanya came over dragging us with her and said, "George, this is Dan and Martha Everheart and they have a request for a performance." We began explaining about the movement to reach out to the Earth and how there was a couple of young people very involved in our group who were getting married. We noticed more and more people were gathering around as we explained our request.

"We are having a celebration of our fourth anniversary of connecting with the Earth and included in the celebration is a wedding on Earth of a couple of young people who were with us from the beginning. This will be the first inter-realm celebration where both sides can see what is happening both on Earth and in the Spirit World simultaneously," I explained. No one here had any idea that this connection with Earth existed and how it had progressed. No one that is, except George, who had received many invitations to meet fans through several of our spirit centers. He had declined all of these requests but he was intrigued with our proposal.

"I have a band here, called White Horse Revival and if you are interested we could put on a test show for you. I grew disgusted with my fame and all the idolization during the later years of the Beatles and never want to perform like that again. But this sounds different, more noble, I guess. I'll let my mates know. What do you think of that?" George said. We were charmed by his British accent right away. Our speech would also be considered closer to an older British accent as we were British citizens in early American history. "Fortunately by performing here in the spirit world I won't be swarmed by screaming maniac little girls who are in love with me and trying to rip my clothes off. Tanya, used to be one of those screaming girls, but she has mellowed and matured and so I let her be here," George continued.

We guessed that Tanya kept herself looking closer to the age she had been when following the Beatles on Earth. It is everyone's own decision what age to appear to others and generally not polite unless you were on familiar terms to ask why they chose a certain age or look. Children who died young would grow to adulthood in spirit world, but you can sense when looking at someone whether they were an ancient spirit regardless of what they looked like. Most people chose to appear to be in their twenties, but some preferred a later time in their life. Martha and I looked more like in our early thirties, perhaps since this was the age that was the most dramatic time for us together right before I died. We really were a team.

It would be easier to bring a small group here to this part of spirit world to see White Horse Revival perform, so we set a date. We would bring Jerry especially who would more likely know whether Patrick and Elsa would enjoy having this band perform. Anselma Glaus would also be invited so she could get the feel of this modern music to integrate it into the overall celebration.

The Celebration

As Thanksgiving approached there was palpable excitement growing, electricity was in the air. HBO was promoting this celebration as a must see event, promising scenes of heaven never seen on Earth, including some secret celebrity performers, some historical reenactments with the actual people representing themselves, out of this world fireworks and on and on. Stations all over the world were making contracts with HBO to link to their show for rebroadcasting at prime times for their locations. Both New Shambles and Shambles World Conferences were working overtime to make the Earth side celebrations and the broadcasts as spectacular as possible.

From the spirit side Anselma had many teams working on preparing different projects. She chose several assistants, people with their own fame and professionalism unquestioned through the ages.

In the higher spirit world if you love certain types of performances, such as; opera, orchestral music, historical reenactments, or plays you would receive a thought invitation of when something was to be performed and then you could attend if you wanted and were free from other important responsibilities. Just as God was reaching out to the Earth through Jiva Satata, He also wanted to reach to different levels of the spirit world, which was millions of times more vast and complicated than the Earth at any time.

With God's love for His children foremost in His heart, God wanted people of other spheres lower than where the celebration was to be held to have a view of heaven. Many billions of spirits had been stuck in their levels through the ages not aware that there was anywhere better or that they could also make progress in their growth towards the realms of light and love. If you believed in eternal damnation and believed yourself damned then your belief alone could keep you from ever going to a higher level. That is the power of thought, the power of belief and that is why we were reaching out to the Earth first, to correct the mistaken beliefs before people go to the spirit world.

God was having spirits in the highest celestial realms send out thoughts to spirits in the gray areas above all parts of the Earth of an event that they could watch that could change their fortunes. This viewing was a grace from God, a gift. Only God could bestow this gift, this vision of heaven to those who had not earned the right to be there yet. The amazing truth was there was room in heaven for every person who had ever been born and that this is everyone's eternal destination however long it takes. The concept of a vengeful God of fire and brimstone was necessary in a more primitive time. But now the truth could be understood, that God is love, God is compassion, God is forgiveness, God is purity, God is all embracing, God is the source of true justice and God is our Father and God is our Mother.

November 28, 2024, Thanksgiving Day, in the bay area of California was colder for this area with a high of 50° but it was clear and refreshing with a slight breeze. The celebration would be a full day event.

Plan for the Celebration

The Pre-Ceremony

The pre-ceremony would be opened by Garuda and Rajinda, with an opening announcement and prayer.

Then there was to be an inter-realm band performance, with musicians in the spirit world playing along with a band on Earth

On the Earth side: Edwin Jackson, Michael Templeton, Jackie Nagorski, Ben Stine, Jill Tanner, Stan and Irene Peterson, and Enrique and Barbara Rodriquez (the Rodriquez's were not part of New Shambles, Inc., but were eagerly invited to the wedding), along with the spirit side: Joseph Fourier, Shirley Jackson, Diane Nagorski, Jerry Tanner and me, put on a skit of the original Thanksgiving meeting four years ago with the Earth side as a live show and the Spirit side projected on a large screen.

Next would be a showing of the first audio/video contact with Jerry Tanner and the dog, Shambles, along with the kids in Edwin's house. Elsa would share how her making a video of her dog, Shambles, and Jerry and posting it on Instagram began the whole exposure of our outreach.

There would be a lunch break with the spirit world lunch displayed on the large screen so the audience could see this informal but natural gathering.

After lunch, an exciting reenactment play in the spirit world would be performed by the actual participants. The skit would be Confucius meeting the emperor for the first time while bravely and very carefully challenging the ethics of the emperor.

Martha and I would then share in an abbreviated form the work we had been involved with Jiva Satata and our outreach to Earth.

A special sharing from Tammy McNeal was next on how her life has changed since her first show that stunned the world.

Juhan and Elif Vaher of Estonia would share their story of their work in Estonia along with showing two videos from their spirit center. All participants on Earth and Spirit World gave permission for these videos.

The Wedding

Finally in the evening, the wedding of Patrick and Elsa would be conducted by Garuda and Rajinda from spirit world, along with Rev. Julie King overseeing the wedding and making it legal on Earth.

Dinner would be served and during the meal there would be entertainment from surprise performers in spirit world.

The celebration would be culminated with fireworks in the spirit world like none ever seen on Earth.

From the spirit side we were all gathered in a beautiful bay overlooking what corresponds to the Pacific Ocean on Earth. Before the actual celebration was to begin, there was a spontaneous show of twenty one dolphins that were leaping out of the ocean in a joyous tribute to everyone there. Garuda, who was robed in a shimmering gold robe walked to a rock that was overlooking the water. Rajinda joined him, beautiful in a pearlescent robe that was flowing from violet to purple to deep blue. Smiling Rajinda said "All of these dolphins were either saved by some people on Earth, saved from fishing nets or predators or they saved people themselves, from ship wrecks or one who saved a child pulled into the ocean by riptides. They are loved forever." Three dolphins popped out together near Garuda and Rajinda dancing backward on their tails chirping their dolphin call. Beautiful sea birds circled close by, sea gulls, pelicans and even some colorful kingfishers.

Then twenty feet away a giant hump back whale popped her head out of the water and gave the shrill call of her kind. She then disappeared and soon emerged from the surface with a full breach, causing a large wave to come crashing to the shore. Garuda and Rajinda were drenched but just as soon were dry again. Garuda let out a hearty laugh and said "This is Valentina and we can't ignore her. She was saved on Valentine's Day 2011 in the Sea of Cortez off Mexico. She is a dear friend of ours. She was entangled in nylon gill fish netting with both her dorsal fins and her tail wrapped tightly. A rescue team cut away the tangles and saved her life. To show her appreciation she then nudged each diver and swam in circles and then in joy put on a show with over forty breaches and tail slaps. She is truly loved and loves all people because they saved her."

To the delight of everyone on Earth this was all shown on their large screen monitors. "Oh my God," said Tammy, "I remember that being on the news! How awesome now she is loved in spirit world. I want to get to know her when I go there." Everyone laughed.

That was the perfect beginning of the celebration that would be seen by millions of people all over the world and in many levels of the spirit world, including, by the grace of God, the gray levels.

Garuda began the introductory speech, "All that you see here is meant for all God's children, this and so much more. Live your life full of love and forgiveness and begin each day giving thanks to God..."

After Garuda's talk there was a full orchestra in the spirit world, with some instruments not familiar on Earth, and they were accompanied with a smaller band on Earth, not having the room for a full orchestra at New Shambles headquarters. They played Matthäuspassion, St. Matthew's Passion, accompanied by a famous American contralto singer, Eula Beal, in the spirit world.

The Thanksgiving skit was very informative to the audience never knowing how this all began four years ago. This was followed by the video that went viral shocking the world with this first view of the spirit realms with Jerry and Elsa's dog, Shambles.

The reenactment play could be displayed as the original spirit participants, Confucius and the Chinese Emperor, projected their historical reenactment into a living performance including their clothes and surroundings that could then be filmed with our spirit cameras and relayed to the Earth counterpart instruments. History students were given a real treat.

The celebration continued with Martha and me sharing our experiences, but this book has been all about that, so no need to go over that again. Next Tammy McNeal gave testimony on how her life has changed from being just a small time talk show host to having her own international company and of her growth through all her contacts with the spirit world. Elif Vaher told of her own transformation from being a popular Estonian television host to running a spirit center with her husband Juhan and running their own show. They cited how Estonia was becoming a more spiritual nation with people meeting friends, family and others who have passed to the next stage of life.

The highlight of the celebration was the first wedding officiated from the spirit world for a couple on Earth and the inter-realm celebration that followed.

The wedding of Patrick and Elsa

During the break, as preparation to begin the wedding was taking place the bi-realm orchestra entertained. Finally a hush fell over everyone as the music became a wedding song, Hava Nagila, in honor of the Stine's Jewish background and also for his ancestors present at the wedding. From the spirit side we were gathered in the Grande Riunioni Hall decorated with a profusion of flowers with the scents intermingling in an intoxicating dance. There was a stone walkway lined with white roses leading to a stage that had a tall arch in the center covered with the most beautiful birds of all colors. First young children came into the hall spreading white rose petals all along the walkway.

Garuda and Rajinda came in next wearing complementary robes that looked like stars and galaxies circling and moving between both robes. Both had crowns of wild flowers and baby's breath flowing down their hair. They stopped at a podium, a redwood sculpture in constant motion as it showed many lives from birth to old age to new birth in the spirit world, a never ending progression.

The inter-realm orchestra began the song Patrick and Elsa chose as their wedding march, "What a Wonderful World" created by Bob Thiele and George David Weiss. On Earth the back doors opened and Benjamin and Ruth Stine accompanied their son, Patrick up to front of the room. Rev. Julie King, robed in a shimmering white robe with a gold tissue faille, sleeve bands, yoke, and hanging stole, was standing next to a marble podium. She had a beautiful smile and her spirit was bright. On the podium were a Torah and a Bible.

Next Elsa and her parents, Jack and Margie, came into the hall. Everyone was transfixed with the beauty of the bride and of the whole ceremony. Elsa, robed in a stunning long sleeve embroidered bridal gown with Queen Anne lace, had tears flowing down her cheeks. Her eyes were like sparkling sapphires shining through the veil as her spirit glowed.

"How many brides wish they could have a marriage like this?" Martha reaching out and holding my hand, whispered to me.

When both families were at the front of the hall the parents left Patrick and Elsa at the altar and took their seats in the front. Rev. King began the ceremony, "Welcome friends, brothers and sisters, in the presence of God we are gathered here for a union of one man and one woman, a union of love and completeness. We are also in the presence of Earth and Heaven and this is one awesome ceremony. I would like to invite our honored hosts in the spirit world to share some words."

Everyone looked at the large screen at the front and Rajinda sweeping her arms out wide and smiling said, "Everyone here is so bright, so full of love. You have brought heaven to Earth on this day. This is an historic wedding, a marriage of a man and woman, of a Jewish man and a Christian woman, a marriage of Heaven and Earth, a marriage of the past that the spirit world represents and the present to make a new future. This is the union of the Yin and the Yang, the masculine and the feminine, the Heavenly Father and the Heavenly Mother representing completeness and new beginning. Rejoice in this day, in this heavenly union!"

Rev. King led the couple in their wedding vows that Patrick wrote for Elsa and Elsa wrote for Patrick. When they were declared husband and wife, (not man and wife which they felt was sexist) Patrick lifted the veil over Elsa's face and kissed her so sweetly, the audience in spirit world and on Earth erupted in cheers and acclamations! All eyes had tears in them, some flowing like a small waterfall.

That night the entertainment mostly from the spirit world was exhilarating. Garuda bemoaned not being able to dance with the bride and I seconded that regret. So we danced with our own wives and then Garuda danced with Martha and I danced with Rajinda.

Valentina, the whale, and twelve dolphins put on a show with synchronized flips and dancing. In spirit world we could feel their joy. There was no trainer here giving them small fish as a treat when they performed correctly. They are intelligent and very aware of what was transpiring.

An ancient Aztec couple in full costume put on a dance that was part of their marriage ceremony hundreds of years ago.

Finally I announced we had a very special performance of someone the couple was familiar with. George Harrison came out with his band, looking like the old Beatles band. Elsa gave a little shriek and Patrick said, "Oh my God!" then apologized for saying God so casually. Martha and I watched with interest, never having an experience of modern bands, so popular with the young and with all ages today.

Mr. Harrison said, "After the Beatles I had my own label, Dark Horse Records and in the spirit world this band is called White Horse Revival, but today me and my mates will be the Beatles for this lovely couple. Our first song for the evening will be Love Me Do."

George Harrison's band played several songs from the Beatles and Martha and I tried to imitate the way Patrick and Elsa were dancing. It was all very foreign to us but we were laughing and having a good time.

Finally the evening ended with a fireworks show like never seen on Earth. Since it is always sunny here in higher spirit world they created an artificial darkness. The performance was orchestrated by the original Chinese cook working in a field kitchen who happened to mix charcoal, sulphur and saltpeter over 2,000 years ago accidently discovering fireworks. For the past two millennium he has perfected his performances. The fireworks revealed dragons, phoenix, stag deer with full racks along with his doe and fawn, people dancing and twirling and so much more. They were like living beings of fire.

Chapter 27
God's Love

The Embrace of Love

Several weeks after the big celebration, Garuda and Rajinda invited Martha and me to their beautiful home in the celestial sphere of heaven to thank us for all our efforts these past few years. We didn't feel we had done enough but deeply appreciated working with Jiva Satata, through all the shows, all the guests, and all the public people we had worked with. Rajinda had prepared some refreshments, some pastries and peach nectar.

After enjoying each other's company, Rajinda reached out to embrace us both and pulled us to her. Garuda also came and embraced all three of us surrounding us with love. "We thank you, our loving God, our Divine Father, our Divine Mother, for Daniel and Martha, for their love and devotion, for their love for you, their love for each other and love for all your children," Rajinda said.

While we were thus embraced a beautiful brilliant white light, an energy force of love, intertwined with golden flashes came down to all four of us and swirled around us. It felt like every cell in my body was filled with love and light. We all started laughing with joy as we were filled with overflowing gratitude and heavenly power. We heard singing harmonized with light and enveloping music like a fountain of joy filling our souls.

A voice both beautiful and mesmerizing said, "Thank you my son, Daniel, my daughter, Martha. Your work will be blessed a thousand fold and will spread to millions and then billions of my sons and daughters. Each person must decide what is true for himself, for herself, I will not decide for them, ever, but you have made it easier for many to find me. Soon we will be one family of love. Look around you, for this beautiful realm is your new home. It is full of the love I have for you, as my gift to you. Share my love with everyone you meet so they can experience my embrace through your love."

Garuda and Rajinda had heard the voice also and all of us had tears streaming from our eyes. I realized that the envelope of protection Rajinda had covered us with so we could be in this higher realm was gone and taking a deep breath felt an intoxicating gush of exhilarating air spread through my body. This was now our home and we could feel God's ever present love. Martha and I hugged each other laughing and crying at the same time. My love for my wife exploded and she could see it in my eyes. She hugged me again and kissed me. We realized we were experiencing the ideal, man and woman together in love with God in the center of our union blending together forever as one pure diamond of goodness. Martha said, "We are home and Samuel is on his way also."

We looked at our friends and I smiled and said, "What is next? There's still so much to do."

Garuda laughing said, "I can see God chose the right people for this work. You never tire and are ready to jump right back into the heart of the work even right after being blessed with God's presence. Well until even one person remains who doesn't know God's love, we have work to do. Helping Earth is the key, because this is where ignorance takes hold and can affect a spirit for thousands of years. Let's go back to your old realm and plan our next move with all of our friends."

And so we did.

References

1. (pg 11) Joseph Fourier http://en.wikipedia.org/wiki/Joseph_Fourier

2 (pg 13) For research in Electronic Voice Phenomenon (EVP) and Trans-Communication read "Miracles in the Storm" by Mark H. Macy and "Conversations Beyond the Light" by Pat Kubis, Ph. D. and Mark H. Macy.

3. (pg 16) Life in the World Unseen by Anthony Borgia; see Chapter 7, "Music"

4. (pg 81) http://en.wikipedia.org/wiki/Budai   According to Chinese history, Budai was an eccentric Chán monk (Chinese: pinyin: chán) who lived in China during the Later Liang (907–923 CE). He was a native of Fenghua, and his Buddhist name was Qieci (Chinese; pinyin: qièc; literally: "Promise this"). He was considered a man of good and loving character.

5. (pg 86) Travels of Marco Polo, http://en.wikipedia.org/wiki/Marco_Polo

6. (pg 93) Belief of Theravada Buddhism, http://www.beliefnet.com/Faiths/2001/06/What-Theravada-Buddhists-Believe.aspx?p=2

7. (pg 110) Papal Infallibility; http://en.wikipedia.org/wiki/Papal_infal-libility

8. (pg 110) Pope Francis; http://www.catholicnews.com/data/stories/cns/1303303.htm

9. (pg 110) Top Ten Popes; http://www.blueguides.com/destinations/italy/rome/history-of-rome-10-top-popes/

10. (pg 118) Gardens created for people in heaven, see: More About Life in the World Unseen by Anthony Borgia

11. (pg 121) Harvard Divinity School; http://en.wikipedia.org/wiki/Harvard_Divinity_School

12. (pg 122) Henry Ware; http://webuus.com/timeline/Henry_Ware. html

13. (pg 122) Unitarian beliefs: http://en.wikipedia.org/wiki/Unitarianism

14. (pg 122) George Whitfield; http://en.wikipedia.org/wiki/George_Whitefield

15. (pg 136) Islamic contributions: http://en.wikipedia.org/wiki/Islamic_contributions_to_Medieval_Europe

16. (pg 137) http://en.wikipedia.org/wiki/Muhammad_ibn_Mūsā_al-Khwārizmī

17. (pg 137) Avicenna: http://en.wikipedia.org/wiki/Avicenna

18. (pg 137) Ali ibn Abi Talib: http://en.wikipedia.org/wiki/Ali

19. (pg 141) See Responsibility, page 404 from Spiritual Light, The Universal Spiritual Brother&Sisterhood

20. (pg 143) See how Hitler is treated in Spirit World in Life in the Spirit World and on Earth by Lee, Dr. Sang Hun (1998)

21. (pg 159) See http://www.faithstreet.com/onfaith/2009/12/30/prophet-muhammads-promise-to-christians/125

22. (pg 180) See http://mv.vatican.va/3_EN/pages/SDR/SDR_00_Main. html

23. (pg 181) https://en.wikipedia.org/wiki/List_of_apologies_made_by_Pope_John_Paul_II

24. (pg 186) See Voices of Love from the Light, Conversation 5, Archangel Michael, page 85

25. (pg 186) See Spiritual Light, Universal Teachings from the Highest Spirit Realms, Chapter 12, Section: Spirit Guides and Spirit Friends

26. (pg 198) https://www.theclever.com/15-famous-ideas-that-were-invented-in-dreams/ and https://www.bedguru.co.uk/goodnight-guru/9-inventions-inspired-by-dreams

27. (pg 198) See page 453, Chapter: Living in the Spirit World, from Spiritual Light, The Universal Spiritual Brother&Sisterhood

28. (pg 198) God is not separate, we were given God's heart, not a copy, the same heart: see "everyday God", the whole book and specifically pages, 99, 95

RECOMMENDED BOOKS

If you are interested in learning more about the Spirit World, the search for truth and our relationship with God, I recommend the following books. These books and more helped prepare for Down to Earth.

CHANNELED TESTIMONIES

Borgia, Anthony (1984). *Life in the World Unseen*. Great Britain: Photobooks (Bristol) Ltd.

Borgia, Anthony (1984). More About Life in the World Unseen. Great Britain: Photobooks (Bristol) Ltd.

Borgia, Anthony (1988). *Here and Hereafter*. Great Britain: WBC Print LTD, Bristol

Cooke, Ivan (1968). *The Return of Arthur Conan Doyle*. Great Briton: Fletcher and Son Limited, Norwich

Farnese, A. (1993). *A Wanderer in the Spirit Lands*. Scottsdale, Arizona: AIM Publishing Company

Hart, Wendy (2011). *The Wider World of Brigeeta Vogall*. Lulu.com ID: 11745740

Kagan, Annie (2013). *The Afterlife of Billy Fingers*. Charlottesville, Virginia: Hampton Roads Publishing Company, Inc.

Lee, Dr. Sang Hun (1998). *Life in the Spirit World and on Earth*. New York, N.Y.: HSA Publications

Lee, Dr. Sang Hun (2001). *Messages From the Spirit World*. New York, N.Y.: HSA Publications

Ritchie, George G. (1978). *Return from Tomorrow*, Grand Rapids, Michigan: Revell Books

Stead, Estelle (2010). *The Blue Island*. Phoenix, Arizona: Mastery Press

Weigel, Jennifer (2007). *Stay Tuned, Conversations with Dad from the Other Side*. Charlottsville, Virginia: Hampton Roads Publishing Company, Inc.

EXPERIENCES WITH GOD

Hose, David and Takeko (2000) *Every Day God*. Hillsboro, Oregon: Beyond Words Publishing, Inc.

Pappalardo, Ronald J. (2013). *Messages from God*. United States: self-published

Pappalardo, Ronald J. and Connie (2015). *Experiences with God, Stories about Mystics: A Guidebook to your own Divine Encounter*. United States: self-published

Walsch, Neale Donald (2006). *Home with God, In a Life That Never Ends*. New York, N.Y., U.S.A.: Atria Books

Walsch, Neale Donald (2004). *Tomorrow's God, Our Greatest Spiritual Challenge*. New York, N.Y., U.S.A.: Atria Books

NEAR DEATH EXPERIENCES

Alexander, Eben (2012). *Proof of Heaven: A Neurosurgeon's Journey into the Afterlife*. New York: Simon & Schuster

Alexander, Eben (2014). *The Map of Heaven: How Science, Religion and Ordinary People are Proving the Afterlife*. New York: Simon & Schuster

Neal, Mary C. Ph.D. (2011). *To Heaven and Back A Doctor's Extraordinary Account of Her Death, Heaven, Angels, and Life Again: a True Story*. Colorado Springs, Colorado: Waterbook Press

Moody, Raymond, A., Jr., M.D. (2010). Glimpses of Eternity, An Investigation into Shared Death Experiences. Great Britain: Ebury Publishing, a Random House Group company

Moody, Raymond, A., Jr., M.D. (1975). *Life After Life.* Covington, Georgia: Mockingbird Books, Inc.

Moorjani, Anita (2012). *Dying to be Me.* United States: Hay House, Inc.

Morse, M.C., Melvin (1990). *Closer to the Light, Learning from the Near-Death Experiences of Children.* United States: Ballatine Books

PSYCHIC AND SPIRITUAL MEDIUMS

Babinsky, Joseph (2015). *Family Reunion, Afterlife Contact.* Arizona: Gentle River Publishing

Betty, Stafford (2011). *The Afterlife Unveiled.* Alresford, Hants, UK.: O-Books

Burley, Philip (2018). *Voices of Love from the Light, Conversations with 20 Great Souls in the Afterlife.* Phoenix, Arizona: Mastery Press

Dresser, Elizabeth Charlotte and Rafferty, Fred (2011). *Spirit World and Spirit Life.* U.S.A.: www.ICGtesting.com

Edward, John (2001). *Crossing Over.* San Diego, California: Jodere Group, Inc.

Ford, Arthur (1968). *Unknown but Known.* N.Y., New York: New American Library, Inc.

Parkinson, Troy (2009). *Bridge to the Afterlife, A Medium's Message of Hope and Healing.* Woodbury, Minnesota: Llewellyn Publications

Robinett, Kristy (2015). *It's a Wonderful Afterlife, Inspiring True Stories from a Psychic Medium.* Woodbury, Minnesota: Llewellyn Publications

Van Praagh, James (2008). *Ghosts Among Us.* New York: HarperCollins Publications

Van Praagh, James (2011). *Growing Up in Heaven.* N.Y., New York: HarperCollins Publications

REVELATORY MESSAGES

Holy Spirit Association for the Unification of World Christianity (HSA-UWC) (1996) *Exposition of the Divine Principle: Principle of Creation*. New York, NY: HSA-UWC

Universal Spiritual Brother&Sisterhood (2014). *Spiritual Light: Universal Teachings from the Highest Spirit Realms*, Cupertino, California: USB Vision Press

SCIENTIFIC RESEARCH INTO ELECTRONIC VOICE PHENOMENON (EVP) AND TRANS-COMMUNICATION

Kubis, Pat Ph.D. and Macy, Mark (2013). *Conversations beyond the Light*. Boulder, Colorado: Griffin Publishing

Macy, Mark (2001) *Miracles in the Storm*. N.Y., New York: New American Library

SPIRITUAL SEARCH AND RESEARCH

Clark, Nancy (2012). *Divine Moments*. Iowa, U.S.A.: 1stWorld Publishing

Clark, Nancy (2012). *Hear His Voice*. Iowa, U.S.A.: 1stWorld Publishing

D'Souza, Dinesh (2009). *Life after Death, The Evidence*. Washington D.C: Regnery Publishing, Inc.

Lees, Robert James (Originally 1898). *Through the Mists, Volume 1*. Prescott, Arizona, U.S.A.: Reprinting by Gentle River Publishing

Lees, Robert James (Originally 1905). *The Life Elysian, Volume 2*. Prescott, Arizona, U.S.A.: Reprinting by Gentle River Publishing

Lees, Robert James (Originally 1931). *The Gate of Heaven, Volume 3*. Prescott, Arizona, U.S.A.: Reprinting by Gentle River Publishing

Lorimer, David (2015). *Prophet for Our Times, the Life & Teaching of Peter Deunov.* Carlsbad, California: Hay House, Inc.

Panchhadasi, Swami (1915). *The Astral World, Its Scenes, Dwellers and Phenomena.* Chicago, Illinois: Advanced Thought Publishing Co.

Pappalardo, Ronald J. (2009). *Reconciled by the Light, the After Death Letters from a Teen Suicide.* United States: self-published

Pappalardo, Ronald J. (2012). *Reconciled by the Light, Book II, Spirit Messages from a Teen Suicide, Adventures of a Psychic Medium.* United States: self-published

Pobanz, Kerry (2012). *Life in Eternity: Human Beings in the Spirit World.* United States: self-published

Singer, Michael A. (2007). *The Untethered Soul, the Journey Beyond Yourself.* Oakland, California: New Harbinger Publications, Inc.

Swedenborg, Emanuel (1976). *Heaven & Hell.* New York, N.Y.: Pillar Books